Preserving Family Lands: Book II

MORE PLANNING STRATEGIES
FOR THE FUTURE

Stephen J. Small
Attorney At Law

Landowner Planning Center
Boston, Massachusetts

The purpose of this book is to alert landowners to the nature and extent of the potential tax and land-saving problems that may face them and their families, and to suggest possible solutions. No reader should undertake any of the suggestions described in this book without first consulting experienced professional advisors.

Tax and family land planning is an individual and personal matter for each landowner and for each family. Current financial circumstances and long-term financial goals differ, as do relationships between family members and different generations. Any single book cannot be, and this one is not intended to be, a substitute for individual tax and legal advice and planning.

Art: © 1996 Christopher Gurshin: Licensed to Stephen J. Small, 1997
Design and typesetting: Marcia S. Miller, *Desktop Design & Publication*

Printed in the United States of America
Library of Congress Catalog Card Number: 96-095381
ISBN: 0-9624557-3-3
First Printing 15,000 copies

Landowner Planning Center
P.O. Box 4508
Boston, MA 02101-4508
Phone: 617-357-1644

Special bulk rates are available for the purchase of **Preserving Family Lands: Book II**. See the order form at the back of the book.

If you would like to be on the Landowner Planning Center mailing list for announcements about publications and other information, please write to us and let us know.

TABLE OF CONTENTS

INTRODUCTION

When I wrote **Preserving Family Lands** in 1988, I wanted to let readers know about some of the tax problems, especially the estate tax problems, faced by landowners. **Preserving Family Lands** has now sold more than 75,000 copies, in all 50 states and abroad, and it's time for another book.

Preserving Family Lands was intended to be an introduction, a "primer." This is the next book in the series. This book is intended to carry that education process a few steps further for landowners, and their families, and their advisors, all of whom may be involved with the planning.

Preserving Family Lands continues to be a good introduction to the field, and if you haven't read it you should. **Preserving Family Lands: Book II** covers a few of the same issues, such as conservation easements and the basic estate tax rules, but it also covers the next generation of planning. This book covers more sophisticated tax planning techniques and concepts. Please keep in mind that **Preserving Family Lands: Book II** is not intended to be exhaustive or all-inclusive, and that in order to keep it relatively easy to read I have had to rely on a number of generalizations about what really are complex issues. That is why the warning to "check with an experienced advisor" appears throughout the book.

A FEW MORE OBSERVATIONS

Planning for your land is a process. Understand this point: the process is not a simple one. But the better informed you are, the easier it is to decide which of the various tools make the most sense for you, for your family, for your land, and for your other assets. This book will try to walk through some of the most significant tax and legal issues a landowner needs to understand to plan intelligently for his or her property. For decades now, business owners have been asking for and have been getting *good sophisticated planning* to protect the family business and to get that asset through the transfer tax system into the hands of the kids. Landowners should be asking for no less and should be getting no less.

Just like the family business, land is an asset. Many readers of this book already want to protect their land and get it to the kids intact. For many other landowners, however, the question "what should I do with my land?" has a whole range of possible answers, all the way from selling it for development to donating all of it to charity. Those readers will want to look at the tax, legal, and land protection techniques presented in this book as helping to frame *one possible economic choice* about their land.

For many readers, not to put too fine a point on it, the clock is ticking. *The principal private landowners in this country are older.* If you do the planning, you can have some say over what happens to your land in the future. If you don't do the planning, your heirs will learn that *the estate tax is high and the cost of doing nothing is high.*

As I did with **Preserving Family Lands**, I would like to thank all of my friends in the land trust community and elsewhere who reviewed earlier drafts of this book. The criticism was thoughtful and the suggestions were constructive. A special thanks to my wife Connie for her invaluable help both in editing my manuscript to keep it readable and in being the general contractor for all of the separate art, design, and printing steps necessary to produce this book. Finally, thanks to Connie and my daughters Stephanie and Victoria for their encouragement and support.

I hope this book is helpful.

S.J.S.

❦ 1 ❦

FOUR FAMILIES

JOHN AND MARY AND RIVERVIEW

John and Mary Landowner are very lucky people. Almost thirty-five years ago they bought Riverview, a 200-acre estate, for $100,000. The value of Riverview crept up steadily for fifteen years after that and then skyrocketed. Even with a recent decline in the real estate market, Riverview is still worth $2 - $2.5 million today.

John and Mary and their three children love the woods, the hills, the open fields at Riverview, the quiet, the sense of calm about the place. They love to go for long walks down its sun-dappled paths at the end of the day or in the early morning hours, when they often spot deer bounding away through the underbrush. They are pleased, and proud, that they have been able to keep Riverview intact. John and Mary are now both seventy.

For years the Landowners have used an attorney (now also a casual social acquaintance) at a local firm for personal and estate planning matters. After brief discussions with their lawyer, they agreed to leave equally to their three children Riverview and the $1,500,000 in other assets they have accumulated. In fact, although John and Mary and the children don't talk about this sort of thing very much, John and Mary have told the children they could each expect a "share" in Riverview and a substantial inheritance. Their wills are on fine, white crinkly paper, with red lines down the margin and a blue binder in the back. The wills were properly executed and witnessed in the lawyer's office, and pleasantries were exchanged. The documents are technically correct in every respect, including a very simple summary sheet at the back of their set of copies of their documents. The summary sheet looks like this:

Total Estate:	$4,000,000
Total Estate Tax Due:	$1,648,000
Balance to Heirs (not including expenses of estate administration):	$2,352,000

John and Mary were uncomfortable when they left their lawyer's office. John and Mary have a gut feeling that they have a problem, but they assume it's not solvable because their lawyer hasn't solved it for them. In fact, he's told them that "everything is taken care of." What the summary doesn't state in bold letters, what the lawyer doesn't acknowledge, and what John and Mary haven't really wanted to think about is this: at the death of the second spouse to die, *Riverview is going to have to be sold to pay the estate tax. The estate planning documents are technically correct but they don't save Riverview.*

We will come back to John and Mary and Riverview later in this book.

SUE AND DIAMOND RANCH

Sue Ranchowner owns Diamond Ranch, 500 acres that her late husband's father bought in the late 1940s for $50 an acre; Diamond Ranch has been owned by the family since that time. All of the family's energy, and almost all of the family's cash, has been poured into the ranch. Sue's husband Bob died a few years ago. Sue is now sixty-eight. Sue and the children love the land. It has saddened them over the years to see other ranches and farms in the area sold off and subdivided; condos now sprout where meadows used to grow. It gives them a real sense of satisfaction to know that they have been able to keep Diamond Ranch intact.

Diamond Ranch is prime ranching and agricultural land on the urban fringe. Even though Sue doesn't feel like she's rich, because of increasing development pressure in the area Diamond Ranch is now worth $1,700,000. Bob and Sue were not able to save much money, but with small inheritances from their parents Sue also has about $150,000 in cash and stocks.

Sue has two married children and four grandchildren. The families are close. Her son lives out of state; her daughter lives nearby. The families have discussed the future of Diamond Ranch. While they all agree the property will pass out of the hands of the family at Sue's death, they also agree they would like to see Diamond Ranch remain in ranching and agricultural use.

Sue and the children love the land. It has saddened them over the years to see other ranches and farms in the area sold off and subdivided; condos now sprout where meadows used to grow.

When Bob died, under his will he left everything to Sue. Under Sue's will, at her death her estate passes equally to her two children. Perhaps a more accurate way to put it is that when Sue dies, after the estate tax is paid Sue's children divide what's left.

Sue has an estate valued at $1,850,000. In every single state, the combined state and federal estate tax on an estate of that size is *at least $500,000;* in many states the total tax is higher than that! It is absolutely clear to Sue that *Diamond Ranch will have to be sold to pay the estate tax.*

We will come back to Sue and Diamond Ranch later in this book.

THE SMITH FAMILY AND SANDY POINT

In the early 1950s Grampa Smith purchased Sandy Point, 2,500 acres of upland and barrier island off the coast. When Grampa Smith died in 1972, he left Sandy Point in four equal shares to his wife Lucy and their three young children, Tom, Sarah, and Patricia, and he left the rest of his rather sizable estate to Lucy. In 1976, Lucy put her one-quarter interest in Sandy Point in a trust. The trust was set up to run for the lives of Tom, Sarah, and Patricia. At the death of the last survivor of the three of them, the trust will terminate and any assets in it will pass equally to their heirs.

The retired lawyer who is still the trustee of the trust Lucy set up believes that Sandy Point should be sold for top dollar, bulldozed, paved over, and subdivided.

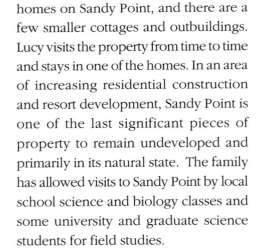

Tom, Sarah, and Patricia all have homes on Sandy Point, and there are a few smaller cottages and outbuildings. Lucy visits the property from time to time and stays in one of the homes. In an area of increasing residential construction and resort development, Sandy Point is one of the last significant pieces of property to remain undeveloped and primarily in its natural state. The family has allowed visits to Sandy Point by local school science and biology classes and some university and graduate science students for field studies.

Lucy's son Tom was divorced from his first wife in 1990. After his remarriage he put his interest in Sandy Point in a corporation and began making gifts of stock to his children. Now, Tom's corporation, the trust, Sarah, and Patricia are all co-owners; each owns a one-quarter interest in Sandy Point. Tom and his family rarely come to Sandy Point. Sarah is married and has four children, and they all are regular visitors. Patricia never married; she and a group of friends regularly come to the property. Patricia has been fairly successful financially.

Tom and Sarah and Patricia knew that the value of Sandy Point was going up over the years, but they had no idea how much. Late last year a nearby 350-acre property, also on the coast, sold for $1,000,000. A local real estate broker has told Patricia she thinks she could get $5,000,000 for Sandy Point.

Sarah would prefer not to sell Sandy Point, and has fond memories of the many years the family has spent there, but she and her husband are looking at mounting expenses as their children grow older. Patricia does not want to sell Sandy Point and believes strongly that it should remain just as it is. The retired lawyer who is still the trustee of the trust Lucy set up believes that Sandy Point should be sold for top dollar, bulldozed, paved over, and subdivided. Tom has said to his sisters that the future of Sandy Point is not up to him.

The future of Sandy Point is not clear. Will Tom and Sarah and Patricia work together? Will Sandy Point be sold? Protected? Developed?

We will come back to the Smith family and Sandy Point later in this book.

ON THE OTHER HAND: SALLY AND PAUL AND SALLY'S SPECIALTIES

Sally and Paul Entrepreneur are very lucky people. Fifteen years ago, Sally began designing a line of home furnishings, selling her products out of her home. Product lines have increased and the business, Sally's Specialties, has grown steadily over the years.

Paul even quit his partnership at an accounting firm to work with Sally because Sally's Specialties needed his management skills. Their eldest child, John, now works for the family business and their younger daughter Victoria is planning to join the business after she finishes business school. Stephanie, their middle child, is a talented actress.

Sally and Paul now own all of the stock of Sally's Specialties. Paul has recently run some of the numbers and believes the business might be worth something in the $4 - $5 million range. Sally and Paul are in their late fifties, and they decide it's time to sit down with their lawyer and talk about the future of Sally's Specialties. They realize that without further planning, they are likely to face an estate tax in excess of $2,000,000, *and that will force the sale of Sally's Specialties.*

After a long conference with Paul and Sally, the family's lawyer is pleased.

...without further planning, they are likely to face an estate tax in excess of $2,000,000, and that will force the sale of Sally's Specialties.

"There's a great deal of planning we can do for you," he says, "and you'll be happy with the results, I know. Our firm does a great deal of succession planning for business owners. Among the arrangements we will need to consider are new wills and trusts for both of you, a shareholders' agreement, possibly a separate buy-sell agreement, stock recapitalization, and purchase of some life insurance.

"As we go forward with these steps, we'll need to review ways to start giving stock to the children, possibly find some way to throw off income to Stephanie, and generally try to move some of the value in the company down to the next generation of ownership.

"Let's go to lunch," the lawyer says. "I can explain some of the techniques we plan to use and some of the basic estate and gift tax rules. There are some simple but fundamental estate and gift tax rules every successful business owner ought to know about. Let me give you this little pamphlet our firm has prepared, '*Family Business Succession: Begin Planning Now.*' I know you'll want to refer to it later."

"I think we're in the right place," Sally says. "But I'm a little concerned this planning effort might be expensive."

"It won't be cheap," their lawyer responds. "But this is the most important asset your family owns. It has brought you financial satisfaction and emotional satisfaction. Without good planning, Sally's Specialties will be gone some day. With good planning, this business can be the cornerstone of your family's security well into the next generation. This is not the time to be penny-wise and pound-foolish."

"Let's go to lunch," Paul says.

WHAT ABOUT THE LANDOWNER? WHAT ABOUT THE LAND?

For decades now, the professional planning community, including the legal community, has devoted countless hours and enormous creative energy to *getting the family business through the estate tax system and into the hands of the next generation of family ownership.* As Sally and Paul Entrepreneur will learn (although not in this book), this is not an inexpensive process, this is not always a simple process, and this is not always a successful process. But there are tools, there are creative approaches, there is a clear recognition of the problem, and there are plenty of professional advisors who know how to approach family business problems and know how to try to solve them. Law firms, accounting firms, brokerage firms, and insurance agencies constantly advertise seminars on "business succession planning" in all its forms.

So much for Sally's Specialties; so much for the business owner.

But what about what may be the most important asset for countless other families? What about the land?

What about Riverview and the family and the community that cares for its gently rolling hills and open fields? What about Diamond Ranch, its tradition of productivity, and its contribution to the ranching and agricultural base? Who solves the problem for Sandy Point, its marshland, open space, and tranquillity? *What about the family or the landowner that cares about the land and wants to see that land protected?*

What about the family that wants to leave its land to future generations?

Where can they turn for help with succession planning for the family's land? What do they need to know? What do *you* need to know?

❧ 2 ❧
WHAT DO I NEED TO KNOW?

THE PRINCIPAL PRIVATE LANDOWNERS IN THIS COUNTRY ARE OLDER

A few years ago I attended a national conference in Montana. One of the speakers made the following observation.

"There are 90 million acres of land in Montana," he said, "and over the next fifteen to twenty years 30 million of those acres are going to change hands. That's because that's how much land we have that is owned by people who are an average age of 59-1/2."

That is really remarkable, I thought. And then I thought, you know, that's true not only in Montana, it's also true in Virginia...and New York...and Florida...and Colorado...and *all over the United States*. The principal private landowners in this country are older, 55 and older, even 65 and older. And over the next fifteen to twenty years, millions and millions of acres around the country are going to change hands, and potentially change use, as these older landowners plan for, or don't plan for, what's going to happen to their land.

I've done a little checking, and although there's not a lot of data on this, I have been able to come up with some statistics. In New England, the average age of the woodlot owner is over 60. In the Southeast, the average age of the private forestland owner is 64. I was told recently that on one particularly important stretch of scenic road outside of Lexington, Kentucky, there are 20 landowners and 18 of them are 70 or older.

In 1988, I wrote another book called *Preserving Family Lands*. The message of *Preserving Family Lands* was simple: if you have a piece of land you care about, you may have a serious estate tax problem. The land may have become so valuable that it may have to be sold to pay the estate tax. *John and Mary and Riverview* and *Sue and Diamond Ranch* in *Chapter 1* are good examples of what I mean. But when you understand that *the principal private landowners in this country are older,* and when you understand the significant estate tax so many of those landowners face, it becomes absolutely clear that millions and millions of acres of open space, wildlife habitat, farmland, forestland, wildlife corridors, watershed, and ranchland *are at risk over the next few decades.*

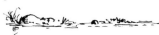

...millions and millions of acres of open space, wildlife habitat, farmland, forestland, wildlife corridors, watershed, and ranchland are at risk over the next few decades.

There was another message in **Preserving Family Lands.** If you are a landowner, and if you care about your land, and open space, and wildlife habitat, and about preserving the quality of life in your neighborhood and your community, you may have an estate tax problem *but you also have some tools for dealing with that problem.* **Preserving Family Lands** provides an introduction to some of the tools. This book will teach you more.

Consider this. What if instead of owning Riverview John and Mary had a successful family business like Sally's Specialties? Would John and Mary and their advisors have done some sophisticated tax, financial, and legal planning to get the family business through the transfer tax system to the children? Absolutely! Like Sally's Specialties, it's likely that there would be a shareholder agreement, buy-sell provisions for the stock, life insurance, a program of annual gifts of stock, and perhaps a stock recapitalization. In short, there is a whole array of entirely appropriate tools to keep that business intact and get it to the kids.

Why haven't John and Mary and their advisors done the same sort of sophisticated, aggressive, creative planning for Riverview? Why hasn't Sue done the planning for Diamond Ranch? "Succession planning for the business owner" is an accepted tax planning and financial planning discipline. For those of us who value open space, wildlife habitat, farmland, forestland, and ranchland, and the outdoor recreational opportunities that come with open land, I think *it's time we begin to focus on tax, legal, and financial planning for family lands. It's time we begin to focus on "succession planning for the landowner."*

What else do you need to know?

YOU CAN'T JUST DO NOTHING

If you care about your land, you need to know that you must act.

You need to know that while "doing nothing" might have worked twenty years ago, or for the prior generation, you can't just "do nothing" any more.

I recall some years ago doing a workshop on estate planning for dairy farmers. I talked about estate tax issues, income tax issues, conservation easements, and tax and legal planning matters. At the end of the program, a woman stood up in the back of the room and asked a question that went something like this.

"Mr. Small," she said, "we just want to be left alone. Our grandparents and our parents loved this farm and loved the dairy business. They had no intention of selling the place. We have no intention of selling the place. Our children plan to follow us into the dairy business and *they* have no intention of selling the place.

"Are you telling us that we're going to have to hire a lawyer, hire an appraiser, maybe hire a surveyor, maybe hire a land use planner, learn all these rules, make all these decisions, come up with all these documents, and pay all these fees—*just to protect our right to be left alone?*"

That's a very powerful question.

I thought a bit. Then I responded.

"You know what?" I said. *"You're right. That's not fair,* but that's the way it is. If you care about your land, you must do something. If you don't plan, the land will be gone."

Pay attention. There are landowners all over this country who don't like to be told what to do with their real estate. Well, my friends, let me tell you something: *if you don't do the planning, Uncle Sam is going to tell your heirs what to do with that real estate, and they aren't going to like what they hear. For the first time in the history of the United States, the family that just wants to leave its land to the children may not be able to do that any more. That land may have to be sold to pay the estate tax.*

That's bad news and good news together. The bad news is that you *can no longer do nothing* if you care about your land. "The system" forces you to act. The good news is that if you do take the right planning steps, if you do the planning for your land and whatever other assets you may own, you can achieve wonderful and satisfying results.

Another observation here. Even if you have already done some planning, or if you believe you have done all of the planning, you still may want to read through this book. There are a lot of planning opportunities, and there are also a lot of misconceptions about tax planning and land planning options.

What else do you need to know?

HOW DO YOU GET THE FAMILY TO AGREE?

You need to understand the planning process. The fundamental issues in **succession planning for the landowner** are the same as the fundamental issues in succession planning for the business owner: value, liquidity, tax planning, and family dynamics.

Simply put, the process involves three fundamental "phases":

- gathering information;

- reaching consensus;

- implementing the plan.

Broken down into more specific parts, here is how the process moves forward.

GATHERING INFORMATION

First, we need to know what the goals are of each family member. This might take meetings, telephone calls, conference calls, and possibly even a questionnaire.

Next, the family needs to know *all* of the relevant tax planning and land planning options. Out of that extensive list, we need to know which ones might be right for this particular family and this particular piece of land. What are the development possibilities and constraints? What are the local market trends? How much is the land worth?

Once the family understands all of the tax planning and land planning options, we need to know if any of the goals change. As part of the learning process, many families have said, "I didn't know we could do that!"

REACHING CONSENSUS

Once we get this far we have reached the heart of the planning: how do we get to consensus? How do we combine the family's goals with the legal rules to get to agreement? What does it take to reach consensus? There are three essential ingredients.

First, the family needs to come to the table willing to learn and willing to agree.

Second, the family's advisor needs to be able to put a menu of choices on the table. To do that, the family's advisor may need to call on other experts who can help develop various elements of a plan.

Third, the advisor needs to understand the process of getting the family to agreement and needs to know how to walk through that process with the family.

Some families are able to reach agreement on current goals, but the planning process can't end there. *Has the family thought about what happens to the property twenty or thirty years into the future?* Does the result envisioned by the current planning process simply put off family issues or problems that might come up in thirty years (like a disagreement over what to do with the property at *that point*)? Does it anticipate those potential issues?

Of course, in some families the landowner or landowners know what they want to do and they are going to go ahead and do it, regardless of what other family members (for example, their children) think. Even in this situation, it is often a good idea to let other family members know what your plans are.

IMPLEMENTING THE PLAN

The third phase of the planning is implementing the plan. What documents are necessary? What specific pieces of work need to be coordinated? What do we need to do to achieve the result the family wants? Does the result create new estate planning opportunities (or issues) for family members? What do we need to do to take advantage of the opportunities?

This book will take a look at the planning process for John and Mary, and for Sue, and for the Smith family. Once you understand some of the basic rules, and the planning process, you may have some sense of how the process applies to *your family.*

What else do you need to know?

THE BASIC RULES

You need to know the basic rules. Just like with a family business, if you have family land you must know a little bit about a whole range of tax and legal issues. This way, you can think intelligently about your choices and you can plan intelligently to reach your goals. That's what this book is for: to cover some of the rules, the concepts, and the process that will be helpful in *planning for your land and in planning for the rest of your assets.*

You need to know how the estate and gift tax rules work. Most people have never, *ever* needed to know anything about the estate and gift tax rules. If you are a landowner, an understanding of a few basic estate tax concepts is essential to be able to plan ahead, for your land and for the rest of your assets. I discuss the estate and gift tax rules in *Chapter 3.*

You need to know something about conservation easements. Protecting and planning for your land often involves a conservation easement. *Chapter 4* will discuss conservation easements.

Chapter 4 will also discuss how a conservation easement can *lower* the value of your land and *save* estate taxes. In addition, *Chapter 4* will cover the income tax rules concerning charitable deductions.

You need to know about trusts, partnerships, and corporations. What is a trust? What is a "family trust"? Should I use a corporation? What kinds of partnerships are there? To get land and value to the next generation (or generations) in the most sensible way and at the *lowest tax cost*, you need to know a little about trusts, partnerships, and corporations (what lawyers call "choice of entity") and how those entities are taxed. *Chapter 5* is on trusts, partnerships, and corporations.

You need to understand the role of life insurance, charitable remainder trusts, private foundations, and planning by will. *Chapter 6* covers these additional tax, legal, and financial planning techniques.

Keep in mind that although these techniques have not traditionally been used in planning for most landowners they are not new techniques. They are *established planning tools* that should at least be on your menu of choices whether or not you own land.

DIAMOND RANCH, RIVERVIEW, SANDY POINT

By the end of *Chapter 6*, you will have a basic understanding of conservation easements, the income and estate and gift tax rules, choice of entity considerations, and some of the other fundamental planning techniques. In *Chapter 7*, we'll take a look at Sue and Diamond Ranch. We will show how by some very *simple planning steps* that rely on the estate and gift tax rules and other planning opportunities covered in the earlier chapters, Sue can begin to make some important decisions about planning for her land and her other assets. In *Chapter 8*, we'll take a look at John and Mary and Riverview again. What's going to happen to Sandy Point isn't clear yet, but in *Chapter 9* we'll take a look at the *planning process* and how it can work in that complex situation.

Again, keep in mind that succession planning for family lands is a process with a lot of different steps along the way. This book has been written to move forward the same way. *Chapter 3* discusses estate tax rules and planning tools, *Chapter 4* covers conservation easements, and *Chapters 5* and *6* go even further along with the process. When it comes to your own planning, you can take the first step only, or some of the steps, or all of the steps. But you need to read the whole book because you need to know what the options are so you can make an intelligent and informed decision about what's right for you.

You could stop reading this book after *Chapter 10*. But if you are interested in some additional planning possibilities and planning tips, you may want to read through the *Appendix* at the end of the book.

❧ 3 ❧
ESTATE AND GIFT TAX PRIMER

THE BASIC RULES

What most people understand about the **estate tax** is that there may be an **estate tax** due when you die. Most people understand that the **estate tax** can be high, although they don't know how high. If an **estate tax** is due, it generally must be paid nine months after death.

Most people don't know too much about **gift taxes**; you *may* have to pay a **gift tax** when you make a valuable gift to someone else.

In order to understand how the various tools work in the planning process, you must know some of the basic rules of the federal estate and gift tax system. Understanding these rules and applying them to your own situation can help you save your land and your other assets.

The federal tax law starts with the proposition that every gift, every *transfer of wealth or value, is potentially subject to gift tax or estate tax.* For purposes of this primer, let's simplify things and let's say we need to understand four important exceptions to this proposition in order to do the planning.

The first exception is the so-called $10,000/$20,000 rule. Under the law, each year you can give away $10,000 to as many different people as you would like *without being subject to any tax.* If you are married, you and your spouse can give away up to $20,000 a year to as many different people as you would like *without being subject to any tax.* You don't pay a tax or get a deduction when you write the check and the money isn't subject to tax for the person who receives it. This is called the "**annual exclusion**." The **annual exclusion**

rules also allow you to pay for medical bills and school tuition costs for others *in addition to* the $10,000 (or $20,000) gifts.

In other words, if you are married and have three children, you and your spouse can give away $20,000 to each child each year (or $60,000 a year, total). Remember that the dollar limitations apply to the *value* of the gift. In other words, if you are married and have three children, you and your spouse can give away $60,000 worth of assets (a vacation home, corporate stock, a farm, a ranch, a painting) each year.

Now, many people I know would like to be able to give $20,000 to each of their children each year but they can't. Some people I know *can* give $20,000 each year to each of their children but they don't want to. But it's remarkable how many people like the idea of giving their children *interests in their land* each year, using the **annual exclusion** rules, to *lower the value of their estates.* We'll discuss this planning step further in later chapters.

The second exception concerns transfers between spouses. Under the federal law, spouses can give each other unlimited gifts, make unlimited transfers of value, either during lifetime or at death, with *no gift tax or estate tax due.* This is called the "**marital deduction**."

The third exception concerns transfers to charity. Transfers to charity have favorable tax consequences. If you give cash, or land, or an easement, or a painting to a qualified charity, you can take an *income tax deduction* and the asset is effectively out of your estate for estate tax purposes.

Here is the last exception. *In addition* to gifts under the **annual exclusion** (the $10,000/$20,000 rule), *in addition* to the **marital deduction** (transfers between spouses), and *in addition* to **charitable transfers**, every individual can give to other people, during lifetime or at death, a total of $600,000 worth of assets *without any federal gift tax or estate tax.* The tax law provision that applies here is called the "**unified credit**."

Here's an example of how this works. Bill, a widower, has $1,000,000 in the bank. Bill gives the $1,000,000 to his daughter tomorrow. There is no gift tax on the first $10,000 of the gift because of the **annual exclusion**. There is no gift tax on the next $600,000 of the gift because of the **unified credit**. There is a gift tax on the remaining $390,000 (the gift tax happens to be $149,100).

Here's another example. Bill has $1,000,000 in the bank. He dies. He leaves the $1,000,000 to his daughter. There is no federal *estate tax* on the first $600,000 because of the **unified credit**. There is an *estate tax* on the remaining $400,000 (the federal estate tax on $400,000 is $153,000; the $10,000 "**annual exclusion**" does not apply once Bill has died). Note that the federal *gift tax* on $400,000 would be $153,000, exactly the same as the *estate tax* on $400,000, because the federal estate tax rates and the federal gift tax rates are *exactly the same*.

Two more observations for this "primer." First, if you make gifts *to grandchildren* or anyone else in that generation or even a younger generation, you should first consult your tax advisor about the **generation-skipping tax**. The **generation-skipping tax** has a critically important $1,000,000 exemption that is comparable to the **unified credit**. You must consult with your tax advisor about the proper and timely use of this exemption.

Second, even though the federal gift tax rates and estate tax rates are the same, there may be significant tax planning advantages to making large gifts (greater than the $10,000/$20,000 **annual exclusion** amounts) during your lifetime. Again, consult your tax advisor.

THE MOST COMMON TAX PLANNING MISTAKE

Now that you understand those rules, let me give you an example of what I think is the *most common* and *most costly* estate planning mistake made by married couples who own land.

Let's assume that John and Mary own Riverview, and that's all they

🌲 *To have a "complete" estate plan, of course, you need a current will, possibly one or more trusts that work in connection with your will, possibly a form of power of attorney, some form of document to address serious illness issues, and possibly more. You need to be aware of complex Medicare and Medicaid rules and you may want to consider insurance to cover long-term medical and care costs.*

own, and Riverview is worth $1,200,000. Let's also assume John and Mary have so-called simple wills, written some years ago: if John dies first, he leaves everything to Mary; if Mary dies first, she leaves everything to John. (Note that for estate tax purposes, the same result will occur if they own Riverview jointly with right of survivorship, or "JWROS" in some states.)

John dies, and he leaves everything to Mary. There is no federal estate tax on John's death because of the marital deduction; he has left everything to his spouse.

Mary dies. She owns Riverview, which is worth $1,200,000. The combined federal and state estate tax is at least $200,000; *this estate tax could have been absolutely, completely, totally avoidable.* Some people I know call this "involuntary philanthropy." Not only that, but because of this planning, or lack of planning, Riverview now has to be sold to pay the estate tax.

Here is what John and Mary could have done; this is a very brief and simplified version of what happens. First, they need to divide up their ownership of Riverview, so they essentially each own half of it. (They could do this, for example, by changing their ownership to "**tenants in common**," a concept we discuss in

Chapter 5). They don't actually have to divide Riverview into two separate tracts of land, but they could do that, too. Then they need new wills that allow them to do the following. Keep in mind that with the appropriate planning documents this works regardless of which spouse dies first.

Say John dies first, and he sets up his estate plan to take advantage of the **unified credit** (which allows him to leave $600,000 worth of assets with no federal estate tax). He leaves his half of Riverview in trust for Mary, so she can use it during her lifetime. The trust terminates at Mary's death and that half of Riverview goes to the children. Because of the **unified credit** there is no estate tax at John's death or when the trust terminates. Mary dies; she owns half of Riverview, and that half is worth $600,000. She leaves her half of Riverview to the children. There is no estate tax at Mary's death because of the **unified credit**. **With these very simple estate planning steps John and Mary have saved more than $200,000 in estate taxes**. Not only that, but because of this planning *they have avoided the forced sale of Riverview.*

THAT'S IT

That's it. Those are the basic federal estate and gift tax rules.

To have a "complete" estate plan, of course, you need a current will, possibly one or more trusts that work in connection with your will, possibly a form of power of attorney, some form of document to address serious illness issues, and possibly more. You need to be aware of complex Medicare and Medicaid rules and you may want to consider insurance to cover long-term medical and care costs. The "complete" estate plan is beyond the scope of this book. In addition, although *most states* follow most of the federal estate tax rules, the estate tax *rates* may be slightly different in some states. Some states have their own gift tax rules. You should discuss all of this with your advisor.

SOME QUESTIONS FOR YOU

Do you have a will? How many years ago did you sign it? Do you know how much estate tax will be due at your death? At the death of your spouse? Do you know what your heirs will have to do in order to pay that tax?

❦ 4 ❦
CONSERVATION EASEMENTS

THE FIRST TOOL IN THE TOOLBOX

For the family that cares about its land, the first tool in the toolbox is a **conservation easement**. With a conservation easement you can *protect your land, lower its value,* and potentially take advantage of *important tax benefits.* Then, using *other planning techniques* you can *move additional value out of your estate,* to children and possibly grandchildren, *for additional estate tax savings.*

More than two decades ago, Congress added the conservation easement provisions to the tax code to provide tax incentives for private landowners who wanted to protect their land. Until more or less the mid-1980s, very few landowners took advantage of this opportunity. Over the past decade, however, conservation easements have become increasingly popular.

BACKGROUND

As a landowner, you have the right to do all sorts of things with your real estate. Subject, of course, to public health and safety laws and zoning requirements, you can put up a forty-story office building on your property, cut down all the trees, dig holes in your property, build condos, put up a fence, and so forth.

A conservation easement is a recorded deed restriction under which you give up some or all of the development rights associated with your property. As an example, what you might say in the easement is, "I reserve the right to live here and come and go as I please. I reserve the right to continue agricultural practices and cut some timber.

Beyond that, there can't be any further development, any more subdivision, or any other commercial or industrial uses." Or you could add, "and I reserve the right to carve out two more five-acre house lots," or three more two-acre house lots, or something like that.

The tax code says you must "give" the conservation easement to a charitable organization (usually in the conservation field) or to a unit of government. But you don't really "give" the donee organization the development rights. The development rights are gone, eliminated, extinguished. What you "give" the donee organization is the right to *enforce the recorded restrictions* on the use of your property, against *you* and *against any future owner of your property, forever.* (There are many important differences between a conservation easement and what people think of as simply a "deed restriction." In most cases it is not at all clear whether a simple deed restriction is enforceable at all or who can enforce it. In a conservation easement, the donee organization enforces the easement and is clearly identified. In addition, a "deed restriction" that does not meet the tax law requirements for conservation easements can potentially create very complex tax problems. In this regard, see the discussion about "Easements or restrictions that don't meet the tax code rules" under #7 of the Appendix.)

...when you restrict your property with a conservation easement, you still own that property.

Remember, when you restrict your property with a conservation easement, *you still own that property.* You can sell the property, subject to the terms of the easement. You can leave the property to your children, subject to the terms of the easement. You can come and go as you please and you are generally free to use the land as you have always used it. In fact, it is usually correct to say that a landowner who cares enough about his or her property to put a conservation easement on it will be doing exactly the same thing on the land *after* the easement is re-corded as he or she was doing *before* the easement was recorded. A properly drafted easement will limit or prohibit activities that are harmful to the conservation values of your property but it will permit you to continue compatible activities.

TAX BENEFITS

When you put a conservation easement on your property, three possible tax benefits can follow if you meet the tax law requirements.

You can lower the value of your property, and that can result in a lower estate tax.

You can take an income tax deduction.

And you *may* be able to lower your property tax.

Let's take each one separately.

ESTATE TAX BENEFITS—LOWERING YOUR ESTATE TAX BILL

In the very vast majority of cases, I believe, landowners who do-nate conservation easements are primarily motivated by three things: they love their land, they love their land, and they love their land. But they are *forced to act* by the looming threat of the estate tax.

Recall that this is what John and Mary are facing. They own Riverview and they have $1,500,000 in other assets.

Total Estate:	$4,000,000
Total Estate Tax Due:	**$1,648,000**

Assume Riverview is worth $2,500,000 unrestricted (again, assume that's what a developer would pay for Riverview). John and Mary put a conservation easement on Riverview, reserving the right to create three more large house lots and preventing any further subdivision or development. Again, and remember this is just an example, let's say the value of most of Riverview as an "estate" that could never be further developed, plus the value of three additional house lots on the balance of Riverview, is $1,200,000.

This is what John and Mary are facing now, with Riverview valued at $1,200,000 and $1,500,000 in other assets:

Total Estate:	$2,700,000
Total Estate Tax Due:	**$939,000**

Obviously, the total estate tax due is still a big number, but *Riverview has been protected* and the *forced sale of Riverview to pay estate taxes* has been avoided.

Another very important thing has happened here, however. By substantially lowering the value of Riverview, John and Mary have begun the process of **succession planning for family lands**. They have set the stage for *additional tax planning steps* (covered in the following chapters) that will make it more likely both that Riverview can pass intact to the next generation and that the family's *other* assets won't be so substantially depleted in the process.

Sue can take that first important conservation and planning step, *but only the first step*, by putting an easement on Diamond Ranch.

Here is Sue's situation now, with Diamond Ranch and her savings.

Total Estate:	$1,850,000
Total Estate Tax Due:	**$520,500**

Diamond Ranch is worth $1,700,000 because that's what a developer would pay for it; the developer would subdivide Diamond Ranch, build homes on it, and sell houses and/or house lots. Assume Sue puts a conservation easement on Diamond Ranch, reserving the right to create only three more large house lots and to continue ranching and agricultural activities, but otherwise preventing any further subdivision or development. The easement reduces the value of Diamond Ranch to its ranching value plus the value of the three house lots; let's say that Diamond Ranch, so restricted, is worth $900,000.

Look at how the estate tax drops, with Diamond Ranch now restricted (including the three house lots that can also be sold to raise cash) plus Sue's savings.

Total Estate:	$1,050,000
Total Estate Tax Due:	**$ 173,500**

To summarize, then, by lowering the value of your property with a conservation easement you can lower your estate tax bill and you can also set the stage for the next planning steps.

INCOME TAX DEDUCTION—LOWERING YOUR INCOME TAX BILL

You can get an income tax deduction for the *value of a conservation easement* that is given to a qualified charitable organization. The value of an easement is equal to the difference in the value of the property before and after it is restricted by the easement.

In John and Mary's case, with Riverview worth $2,500,000 before the easement and $1,200,000 after the easement, the value of the easement is $1,300,000. For Sue, with Diamond Ranch valued at $1,700,000 unrestricted and $900,000 subject to the easement, the value of the gift is $800,000. John and Mary have an income tax deduction of $1,300,000. Sue has an income tax deduction of $800,000.

It is important to understand that when you make a gift of *property* (land, or an easement) to charity, the *value of the gift* may generally be deducted *only up to 30% of the donor's income for the year of the donation*. (Under the tax code, the rule actually is 30% of income subject to certain adjustments. To keep things simple, this book will simply say "income.") Any amount of the deduction remaining after the first year can be carried forward and deducted against income in the five following years. A gift of *cash* to a qualified charitable organization can be deducted up to 50% of the donor's income for the year, again with a five-year "carryforward" of any unused amount.

If Sue has an income of $40,000, and makes a gift of a conservation easement worth $800,000, her deduction in the first year is $12,000 (30% of $40,000). The balance of the value of the gift carries forward for five years. Any deduction not used up is lost.

If John and Mary have an income of $200,000, and if they make a gift of a conservation easement worth $1,300,000, their deduction in the first year is $60,000, or 30% of their $200,000 income. The balance of the gift, $1,240,000, can be carried forward for five more years. With the same $200,000 income, if they instead make a cash charitable contribution of $1,000,000, their deduction in the first year is $100,000, or 50% of their income; the $900,000 balance of the cash gift also carries forward for five more years.

Example 1. John and Mary have an income of $200,000. They make an easement donation with a value of $1,300,000. To keep this very simple, assume they have no other itemized deductions. The tables below are for "Year 1," or the year in which they make the gift. Remember that any amount of the value of the gift they don't use up in "Year 1" can be carried forward and used against their income in five more years. Note also that with $200,000 of income, you would expect to see $60,000 in deductions (30% of their $200,000 income) in the "With the Donation" table below. However, because of limitations in the tax law that reduce itemized deductions for higher-income people, John and Mary's deduction is reduced to $57,538. Later in this chapter, in Sue's case, we will see the same limitations do not apply. Note that the full $60,000 is considered used up for purposes of figuring the amount that can be carried forward.

WITHOUT THE DONATION	
Year 1	
Income:	$200,000
Tax Due:	**$52,614**
WITH THE DONATION	
Year 1	
Income:	$200,000
Deduction:	$57,538
Tax Due:	$34,778
Income Tax Savings (over six years):	**$107,016**

Example 2. Sue has an income of $40,000. Assume she donates an easement with a value of $800,000. Again, to keep this simple, assume she has no other deductions.

WITHOUT THE DONATION	
Year 1	
Income:	$40,000
Tax Due:	**$6,246**
WITH THE DONATION	
Year 1	
Income:	$40,000
Deduction:	$12,000
Tax Due:	$4,006
Income Tax Savings (over six years):	**$13,440**

Four observations. First, most landowners who donate conservation easements cannot "use up" all of the income tax deduction because of the 30%-of-income limitation. They are *not* primarily motivated by the benefits of the income tax deduction (and the above examples certainly tend to indicate why). They *are* primarily motivated by a love of their land and a looming estate tax problem. But the income tax benefits *are there and they are real and they represent real after-tax savings and more dollars in your pocket. Good planning can make maximum use of these tax benefits.*

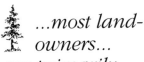

...most land-owners... are primarily motivated by a love of their land and a looming estate tax problem.

Second, another possible way to maximize the income tax benefits could involve the following approach. Instead of John and Mary donating one easement on all of Riverview, John and Mary could donate a first easement on a *portion* of Riverview, carry forward the deduction until it is used up (or until the five-year carryforward ends), and then donate another easement on the rest of Riverview. Sue could do the same sort of planning with Diamond Ranch. This may result in significantly higher income tax benefits over the long term. As with many other planning choices, there are a variety of issues that come up with this technique; check with your advisor.

Third, with tens of thousands of dollars in income tax savings potentially at stake, it is not only *worth it* to pay for good tax advice, it is *important* to pay for good tax advice.

Fourth, with regularly changing tax rates, deduction limitations, and other tax law variables, generalizing about income tax savings from charitable contributions is not very safe (other than the generalizations in the preceding paragraphs, of course...). Don't guess! **Run the numbers!**

PROPERTY TAX REDUCTION—LOWERING YOUR PROPERTY TAX BILL

The gift of a conservation easement will reduce the value of land, often considerably. It would stand to reason, then, that the property tax bill for that land should also drop.

Property tax assessment, however, is up to the local assessors. I have heard many examples of assessors who were responsive to the effect of a conservation easement and reduced a landowner's property tax bill (in some cases, up to 75% to 90%). I have also heard examples of assessors who were not so responsive, often because they did not like conservation easements or because they did not understand conservation easements.

Check with your advisors. In some states (although very few), *under state law* local property taxes must reflect the effect of conservation easements. In some states there are court decisions that hold that when the value of property is reduced by a conservation easement, the property tax assessment should also drop, generally by a similar percentage. But this is a matter you have to take up with city hall.

TAX LAW REQUIREMENTS

To be entitled to federal tax benefits for putting a conservation easement on your property, there are a number of federal tax law requirements. For this chapter, I want you to keep in mind four of them.

The easement must be *perpetual. Forever.* An easement that by its terms is for ten years, or thirty years, or fifty years, *will not* meet the tax law rules for deductible easement gifts (and may cause some very tricky tax law problems, as noted in #7 of the *Appendix*).

The easement must meet a "conservation purposes" test. More on that below.

The easement must go to a "qualified conservation organization." More on that below.

You must have a "qualified appraisal." More on that below.

THE "CONSERVATION PURPOSES" TEST

A few years ago, I received a telephone call from a man in a southern state with the following question.

"I own 100 acres of riverfront property," the caller said. "Under local zoning, I could probably get 88 houses on it. If I do that, the property is probably worth, say, $500,000. Or, I could create 19 five-acre house lots. If I do that, the property is probably worth $450,000.

"My accountant tells me that if I put a conservation easement on the property, and restrict it to five-acre house lots, I can get a tax deduction for $50,000. Is that correct?"

That is probably not correct, I told the caller.

As a rule, the following generalization works: the more significant the land is, the more it adds to the public good, the more likely it is that you will qualify for the deduction.

The tax law in this area says that you must first meet the "conservation purposes" test. Once you do that, once you achieve some significant conservation results with your easement, *then* the tax law allows you an income tax deduction for any value you have given up.

I told the caller that I didn't think carving out nineteen 5-acre house lots on a 100-acre piece of land would meet the conservation purposes test. That may result in a more attractive setting than 88 one-acre lots, I told him, and you personally may believe that the large-lot subdivision is a nice thing for you to do. But you don't get a tax deduction for doing it that way. Just requiring bigger lots does not result in enough significant conservation of the overall 100 acres.

As a rule, the following generalization works: the more significant the land is, the more it adds to the public good, the more likely it is that you will qualify for the deduction. If you are protecting a large tract of primarily undeveloped property (like John and Mary) or ranchland or farmland (like Sue), or a smaller parcel of land with scenic or open space qualities, if you are protecting habitat for an important or threatened animal or plant species, if you are preserving a scenic view on a long stretch of roadside that is threatened with subdivision, if you are contributing to a greenbelt around a city or preserving a watershed of a scenic brook or river or lake, your donation is more likely to qualify for a deduction. In addition, you can meet the "conservation purposes" test if you protect important historic property.

The way the *tax law rules* generally put it, you can meet the conservation purposes test if your donation is:

- to preserve land for public outdoor recreation or education;

- to protect important relatively natural habitat;

- to preserve a scenic view for the general public;

- to preserve open space pursuant to a "clearly delineated" governmental policy; or

- to protect historic property.

You will probably *not* qualify for a deduction if there is nothing special or unusual about the land that you are protecting except that it does not currently have more houses on it. Think of it this way. *If you are truly contributing something to the general environmental well-being of the area, then that's a good (and most likely deductible) gift.* If you are truly trying to get away with something ("maybe I can get a deduction for not permitting any more development on my suburban house lot"), and there is nothing particularly unusual about your property or its setting, you are probably not entitled to an income tax deduction. (As a practical matter, in this latter case it may be difficult to find a donee organization to accept your easement gift. See later on in this chapter.)

Certainly, this is a subjective area, and the "conservation purposes" analysis is not clear in every case. If you don't know whether an easement on your land will meet the conservation purposes test, the donee organization you have in mind for your easement should be able to help you answer this question.

PRESERVING YOUR LAND; PRESERVING INCOME

Some landowners are willing to restrict their land with a conservation easement and give up value simply in order to keep their land looking nice. Other landowners, however, are coming to recognize that a conservation easement in many cases can do more than that. In many cases a conservation easement can *prevent the maximum possible economic exploitation of land, keep land looking nice, and still permit traditional income-producing land uses.* Conservation easements can protect farms and still permit continued agricultural activity. Conservation easements can protect ranches and still permit traditional ranching uses. Conservation easements can protect forestland and still permit prudent timber management and harvesting. Conservation easements can permit limited residential development and even commercial hunting and fishing subject to carefully defined limitations.

> *In many cases a conservation easement can prevent the maximum possible economic exploitation of land, keep land looking nice, and still permit traditional income-producing land uses.*

In fact, in an increasing number of cases, easements permit a variety of income-producing activities on the same property (for example, continued agricultural and forestry activities and some additional limited development), but *still prevent the land from being bulldozed and paved over.*

THINKING ABOUT EASEMENTS

Every landowner is unique; every piece of land is unique. Every single conservation easement should be tailored to meet the needs of *that particular landowner, that particular piece of land, and the area in which the land is located.* The terms of an easement protecting southern bottomland hardwoods and allowing commercial hunting and fishing in the Mississippi Delta are not going to be the same as the terms of an easement to protect natural undisturbed habitat on a beloved family parcel in the northeast. An easement on three acres on the Maine coast is not going to read the same as an easement on a Wyoming ranch. An easement on a South Carolina plantation is not going to read the same as an easement on forestland in Oregon.

...economic issues may be different for each owner and the land use concerns may be different for each owner.

In fact, the terms of an easement on one important tract of forestland in Georgia may not even be the same as the terms of an easement on *another* important tract of forestland in Georgia. The economic issues may be different for each owner and the land use concerns may be different for each owner. A good part of both easement documents *can* be the same; there are some standard or "boilerplate" provisions that generally don't need to be varied. But most of the *substantive land use rules* in both documents could conceivably be quite different.

As a landowner, it is important for you to think these issues through.

What activities do you want to *prohibit* on your land in the future?

What kinds of things are you doing on your land now that you want to be able to continue?

What other activities might you want to do in the future, or permit future owners of your land to do in the future, that are compatible with the conservation purposes of your easement? That will allow the land to be economically viable in the future?

Are you certain that the easement document is clear about what it permits and what it prohibits?

Have you thought about what might happen to your land twenty or thirty years into the future?

Keep this in mind: the conservation easement document affects the use of your land *now and forever.* It is a *perpetually enforceable contract.* The conservation easement document will require a lot of thought on your part, and you shouldn't be in a hurry to make these decisions. In the end, to the extent possible the conservation easement should reflect *your* goals and *your* desires for what *you* want to happen to *your* land.

...when you give a conservation easement... you are giving the donee organization... the job of monitoring and enforcing the terms...in perpetuity.

DONEE ORGANIZATION

The tax law requires that the donee organization be a "qualified conservation organization," and this generally means a charitable organization (usually in the conservation field) or a unit of local or state government or the federal government. Keep in mind that when you give a conservation easement to a donee organization, what you are giving the donee organization is the *job of monitoring and enforcing the terms of the conservation easement* in perpetuity. You can expect that the donee organization will request or insist on certain terms in the conservation easement document to be able to ensure that the conservation values of your property will be protected.

You should certainly be mindful of this responsibility when you choose a donee organization to hold your easement. An organization that doesn't know (or care) much about your land may not be a good choice; an organization that understands how you think about your land and the relevant land use issues is likely to be an excellent choice. In addition, an easement that has been carefully and thoughtfully drafted will include a list of permitted (and prohibited) land use practices, but times change, people change, and landscapes change. You need to be comfortable that you (and possibly your heirs) can establish a good and very long-term working relationship with the donee organization.

In most cases, the donee organization will turn out to be a state or local land trust, that is, a tax-exempt organization involved in land conservation and open space protection. Most land trusts around the country have as their primary purposes the protection of locally important open space, wildlife habitat, scenic property, farmland, forestland, or ranchland. Your local (or statewide) land trust should be happy to hear from you if your land has these or other important conservation values and you are interested in donating a conservation easement that protects these conservation values.

...an easement that has been carefully and thoughtfully drafted will include a list of... land use practices.... You need to be comfortable that you...can establish a good and very long-term working relationship with the donee organization.

Just as examples, the Delta Environmental Land Trust Association, or D.E.L.T.A., accepts easements in Mississippi, Louisiana, and Arkansas. The Vermont Land Trust and the Utah Open Lands Conservation Association accept easements anywhere in their respective states. The Aspen Valley Land Trust takes easements in the Aspen, Colorado, area. Some regional or national organizations hold easements, such as The Nature Conservancy, the Audubon Society, the American Farmland Trust, Ducks Unlimited, the Rocky Mountain Elk Foundation, and the National Trust for Historic Preservation. And there are certainly other tax-exempt organizations, generally in the resource protection business, that currently hold easements or could in the future.

The best source for information about land trusts around the country is the Land Trust Alliance, the national organization of local and regional land trusts. The Land Trust Alliance also has a variety of helpful publications, including *The Conservation Easement Handbook*, *Appraising Easements*, *Conservation Options — A Landowner's Guide*, and *The Federal Tax Law of Conservation Easements*. You can call the Land Trust Alliance at 202-638-4725, or write to Land Trust Alliance, 1319 F Street, N.W., Suite 501, Washington, DC 20004-1106.

Landowners sometimes ask what happens if a land trust or other donee organization holding easements goes out of business in the future. In every state, the attorney general's office has some oversight responsibility for charitable organizations. It is reasonable to assume that if a charitable organization holding easements goes out of business, monitoring and enforcement responsibility for the easements would be assigned to another, similar organization or possibly to a government agency. Some landowners have chosen to designate in the easement one or more "backup" donees to deal with this possibility.

Publicly-Supported Charity or Private Foundation

One important tax law requirement is that the easement holder *cannot* be a so-called "private foundation" or "private operating foundation." Very briefly put, there are generally two categories of tax-exempt organizations, the "publicly-supported" charities and the private foundations. A publicly-supported charity must establish (under certain tax law requirements) that it has a broad base of public financial support. A private foundation is generally funded by a small group of individuals, or a family, or even one person (or even a single corporation). See *Chapter 6* for a further discussion of private foundations.

Almost every land trust in the country is classified as a publicly-supported charity. As an easement donor, however, you should take care to verify that the donee organization for your easement is not classified as a private foundation (or a "private operating foundation") and is otherwise an eligible easement holder. You can do this by reviewing a copy of the letter the charity received from the IRS (a "determination letter") on the charity's tax-exempt status.

As an easement donor... you should take care to verify that the donee organization for your easement is not classified as a private foundation...and is otherwise an eligible easement holder.

Endowment or Stewardship Fund

As noted earlier, when a charitable organization accepts a conservation easement, it accepts the responsibility of monitoring and enforcing that easement in perpetuity. If a land trust or other donee organization is not *willing* to accept that responsibility, or is not *able* to accept that responsibility, it should not be holding conservation easements.

Carrying out that responsibility will cost a donee organization time and money every year. Most (if not all) land trusts recognize this, and as part of the process of reviewing, negotiating, and accepting an easement a land trust will also request a contribution from the landowner to an "endowment" or "stewardship" fund. Generally, this is a permanently restricted fund, and the money is invested so that the income will cover the cost of monitoring and enforcing easements, as well as growing to offset inflation.

Some landowners are not happy about the idea of writing a check to the donee organization *in addition to* donating a valuable conservation easement. However, for an easement to be meaningful the donee organization must enforce the easement and that costs money. Simply put, a donee organization must recognize its stewardship responsibilities and must be certain it can meet those responsibilities.

"QUALIFIED APPRAISAL"

The best insurance against a bad IRS audit experience is a really good appraisal.

Under the tax law, any person who makes a charitable contribution of property with a claimed value in excess of $5,000 *must* have a **"qualified appraisal."**

In general, and simply put, the qualified appraisal rules require that the appraisal be prepared by a thorough, honest, competent appraiser, who understands how to appraise conservation easements.

A "qualified appraisal" must include, among other things, a description of the property, the method used to determine its value, information about the appraiser's qualifications, and a description of the fee arrangement between the donor and the appraiser.

In addition, there are a number of other generally technical requirements you and the appraiser must comply with; check with your advisor for details. The regulations also specify deadlines for when the appraisal must be completed. The tax rules require that the person making the contribution file an IRS Form 8283, Noncash Charitable Contributions, along with his or her tax return for the year in which the gift was made.

In addition to the practical requirement that an appraiser be hired, the earlier a donor has an idea of what the value of the contribution will be, the more opportunity will exist for tax planning that might be advisable in the year of the gift. For a donor who is considering reserving some future development rights, consultation with a good appraiser and an early review of the different value possibilities may be useful. In addition, an appraiser who understands conservation easements may be able to offer other useful suggestions as part of the planning process.

...the earlier a donor has an idea of what the value of the contribution will be, the more opportunity will exist for tax planning....

One further word about the appraisal. If *you* read the appraisal, see a few pages of numbers and pictures, read the appraiser's conclusion, and say "What? How on earth did the appraiser reach that result?", you can be sure the IRS will have the same reaction. If instead you read the appraisal, review and agree with the comparable sales the appraiser has selected, follow the appraiser's methodology, and understand how the appraiser reached that particular result, so can the IRS!

This is a generalization, but it will stand up. By and large, **there seem to have been very few unreasonable attacks by the IRS on conservation easements in recent years**. I understand from the director of one statewide land trust that the trust has accepted approximately 100 easements in the last three years and, to his knowledge, only three of them have been audited. In the mid-1980s, some particular parts of the country had difficult audit experiences with conservation easements, and some IRS agents seemed to be ill-informed about this important tax law incentive, but those experiences mostly seem to have passed. Seeing to it that your **qualified appraisal** is thorough, clear, and persuasive can only help.

FINAL COMMENT ON THIS CHAPTER FROM A LANDOWNER

"Do you know what I did? I protected my beautiful property and I saved it for all the ducks and geese and waterfowl. I lowered the value of my property and now I can leave it to my kids. You should tell more people about this!"

❧ 5 ❧
CORPORATIONS, PARTNERSHIPS, TRUSTS

"I'M READY FOR THE NEXT STEP"

"I'm ready for the next step," you might say now. "Now that I know the estate and gift tax rules, and now that I understand about conservation easements, how do I start getting my land to the children? How can I save more estate tax? Should I put my land into a **corporation** and give shares to the children? What about a **partnership**? What's a 'family trust'? Should I put my land into a **trust**? What about one of those trusts to 'avoid probate'? Should I just deed interests in my land to the children?"

For landowners who want to move ahead with the planning, those are among the most common questions. This chapter will try to sort out some of the information, point out some of the misinformation and common misconceptions, and point you in the right direction.

Once again, keep in mind that we have not yet put all of the pieces together; we will do that in the next few chapters. But in order to put the pieces together properly, we need to know a few more rules.

Also keep in mind that the purpose of this book, and the purpose of this chapter, is to give you a *very brief overview of some of the rules that can be important and useful in the planning process.* Here are some of the things this chapter will cover.

Why shouldn't you use a corporation?

What happens when a corporation sells family land?

What happens when a partnership sells family land?

What is a general partnership? A limited partnership? An S corporation? A limited liability company?

Does putting your land into trust take care of everything?

What are some of the questions you need to talk over with your family and your advisor about partnerships and trusts?

The material covered in this chapter is complicated, and you must check with an experienced competent professional advisor to learn more about this material and these rules and how these planning opportunities might work best in *your particular situation.*

To set the stage for a discussion of the rules, let's use this very brief description of a **corporation**. A corporation is a *separate legal entity* set up by one or more people to carry on a business. The *corporation* may own or buy assets: land, buildings, the products and machinery of the business. The *shareholders* or *stockholders* who own shares of stock are the "owners" of the corporation. The shareholders who set up a corporation can give assets (land, buildings, etc.) to that corporation, and the corporation becomes the owner of those assets. A corporation can have one shareholder or many shareholders. Each state has its own statutes that govern the formation of corporations within that state.

To a significant extent, a working description of a **partnership** sounds a lot like a description of a corporation. A partnership is an organization of two or more persons who have agreed to pool their efforts in a business and to divide the proceeds. Again, the *partnership* may own assets, such as land or buildings; the *partners*, who own *partnership interests*, are the "owners" of the partnership. The partners who set up a partnership can give assets to the partnership (land, buildings, etc.) and the partnership becomes the owner of those assets. Each state has statutes that govern the formation of partnerships in that state.

As a practical matter, the most important difference between a corporation and a partnership turns out to be *how they are taxed.* More on this below. (We'll save the discussion of S corporations, limited liability companies, and trusts until later in this chapter.)

That having been said, let me make this chapter simple.

THIS CHAPTER MADE SIMPLE

Never, never, never put family land in a corporation.

There are exceptions to that rule, but I do not want you to think about the exceptions. I want you to think about the rule.

Never, never, never put family land in a corporation.

Never, never, never put family land in a corporation.

CORPORATIONS AND PARTNERSHIPS

When a **corporation** sells an asset, the *corporation pays tax.* When the money comes out to the shareholders, the *shareholders pay tax.*

The single most important reason why you should not put family land in a corporation is this "**double tax**." There are other ways that you can begin to transfer value to the children and the grandchildren without having to worry about this double tax.

When a **partnership** sells an asset, the *partners pay tax.* In other words, in a **partnership** there is only one tax.

Example 1. Assume that Family Corp. owns Farmacres, and Bonnie and her two children own all the shares of stock of Family Corp. Family Corp. sells Farmacres for $1,000,000. Assume that the federal *corporate* tax on the gain is $316,000.

After the federal *corporate* tax is paid, $684,000 in cash is left. Assume that is paid out in equal shares to Bonnie and the children;

Bonnie and the children must also pay income tax on that money. The *additional federal income tax* on the money that is distributed to Bonnie and the children could total approximately $189,000. Out of the original $1,000,000, then, the family is now left with less than $500,000, and this *does not include any state tax* that must be paid on the corporation's gain or on the money paid to the shareholders.

To summarize:

Sale price:	$1,000,000
Federal tax on Family Corp:	$316,000
Cash distributed to shareholders:	$684,000
Approximate total income tax on shareholders:	$189,000
Balance of cash for shareholders:	**$495,000**

Prior to 1986, the tax laws would have allowed Family Corp. to sell Farmacres for $1,000,000, and distribute the proceeds to Bonnie and the children with only *one tax.* The Tax Reform Act of 1986 changed all that and imposed the so-called "**double tax**" on corporations that is the law today. Even if a corporation simply distributes property to its shareholders (instead of selling it), tax will be triggered if the property has increased in value over its cost to the corporation.

Compare this result.

Example 2. Family Partnership (with three equal partners) owns Farmacres. Farmacres was originally purchased for $100,000 and is sold for $1,000,000. There is a gain of $900,000 but there is *no federal tax on the partnership.* The *partners,* Bonnie and the children, pay federal income tax that could total approximately $240,000. (Again, this is without calculating state income tax.) ***The federal tax savings alone amount to more than $250,000.***

To summarize:

> Total federal tax on $1,000,000 sale
> by Family Corp.: $505,000
>
> **Total federal tax on $1,000,000
> sale by Family Partnership: $240,000**

If Farmacres were sold for $5,000,000 instead of $1,000,000, the total federal tax savings by using a partnership rather than a corporation *would be more than $1,000,000.* Keep this in mind. A corporation may be the traditional entity for "doing business." *For tax reasons it should not be the traditional entity for holding family land.*

More About Partnerships

In a **general partnership**, all partners are "general partners." If the partnership is sued or runs into financial trouble, all general partners are responsible for the debts of the general partnership. Under law, *each general partner has equal management rights in the partnership, regardless of that partner's percentage interest, or "ownership," in the partnership.* In other words, all general partners have the right to sign checks for the partnership, incur liabilities for the partnership, and generally represent the partnership in connection with its dealings with the outside world.

On the other hand, even though these rights are generally given as a matter of law, a partnership agreement can be written that will modify or take away these rights. In effect, the other general partners can agree, in a partnership agreement, that *one of them* (or perhaps more than one) *will have the authority to act on behalf of the others in the partnership in various matters.*

A **limited partnership** consists of one or more general partners and one or more (usually more than one) limited partners. Under partnership law, *limited partners have no say in the management of* *the partnership or the business of the partnership.* The general partners have full authority and obligation to make all decisions, pay bills, and *run the partnership.* Limited partners also are not financially liable for future costs or expenses of the partnership, unless the limited partnership agreement specifically provides otherwise. Like shareholders in a corporation, *they have "limited liability."* That is, they can lose any value they may have in the limited partnership, but their "liability" can't go any further than that. *The general partner (or partners) has the full responsibility to make good on partnership debts,* even beyond the general partner's stake in the partnership.

As a general rule, and this is subject to change in different situations, if a family anticipates that many younger-generation family members may be given interests in the property over an extended period of time it seems to make more sense to use a *limited partnership.* As with corporations, each state has requirements that must be followed to be sure a partnership is properly organized and on record. Particularly with respect to the limited liability that limited partners have, most (if not all) states require that a certificate of limited partnership be filed and on record in a state government office, often corresponding to the Secretary of State.

The legal rules about establishing a valid partnership are one thing; the "business deal," or the arrangement among the partners, is something else entirely.

Keep this important point in mind. The legal rules about establishing a valid partnership are one thing; the "business deal," or the arrangement among the partners, is something else entirely. Writing a standard or "boilerplate" partnership agreement that is valid and enforceable is easy and takes very little time. Having a partnership agreement *that reflects the "deal points" and desires of a particular family* may not be so simple. While the specifics will vary from family to family, here are some things to think about. Of course, these issues may be relevant whether you use a partnership, or an S corporation, or a limited liability company, or a trust.

Some Things to Think About

Who is in charge? Who makes the decisions? What happens when they die, or don't want to be in charge any more?

How many family members are ultimately going to be involved? A few owners? Spouses? Lineal descendants? Grandchildren?

Will there be new structures built on the property *for the use of the family*? For potential sale to an outsider? Is some of the property going to be used quite a bit, while other portions of the property remain relatively natural or wild?

Will the property require substantial repairs or improvements over the years? What will that cost? Will all of the anticipated owners be able to pay? What if all owners are required to pay but one of the limited partners doesn't contribute his or her share? Can't contribute his or her share? Who pays if the money runs out? Should an "endowment fund" be set aside for the family now, to help with future expenses?

Should family members (or others) pay rent if they use the property?

Will the property stay in the family and be used by the family for generations to come? Is there talk of using the property for five or ten years and then selling it? Will a fight loom over this issue? Are there some or many family members who may come to own an interest in the property (simply as a matter of fair division of the family's wealth) who simply will not be interested in using it?

What if a partner wants to get out? Can partners sell their interests? To whom? For how much? Will family members have rights of first refusal?

Who can decide to sell the property?

S CORPORATIONS

Many people ask about "**S corporations**," also often known as "**Subchapter S corporations**." An S corporation is the same as a "regular" corporation except that the corporation is taxed under a special set of rules in Subchapter S of the Internal Revenue Code. ("Regular" corporations are generally taxed under Subchapter C of the Internal Revenue Code, but for tax purposes they are usually referred to as "corporations," not as "C corporations.")

Mostly, **S corporations** are taxed like partnerships. That is, in most cases income earned by S corporations is taxed *only once, to the shareholders.* There are some important situations in which income earned by an S corporation is *also* subject to *corporate* tax; check with your advisors on this point. However, for planning purposes, there is at least one potentially serious drawback to using an S corporation: *the tax law has limits (recently expanded) on who can be shareholders of an S corporation.*

♦ A **corporation** generally *cannot be a shareholder* of an S corporation.

♦ A **partnership** *cannot be a shareholder* of an S corporation.

♦ Some kinds of **trusts** *cannot be shareholders* of an S corporation.

In many cases an **S corporation** makes sense for a business that makes a product and makes money (like Sally's Specialties). But where the asset in question is the family land, and especially when the goal in question is to keep that family land generally intact and in the hands of the family perhaps *for generations to come*, an **S corporation** is often not the best choice. The **S corporation** tax rules can be difficult to work with, and the restrictions on who can own shares in an **S corporation** limit the planning and limit the flexibility.

LIMITED LIABILITY COMPANIES

All states now have laws that allow you to form a "**limited liability company**" or "LLC." An LLC is simply *another form of legal entity* that people have chosen for purposes of doing business and dividing the proceeds. Like a corporation or a partnership, an LLC may own or buy assets, and the LLC is owned by the members or owners who own interests in the LLC.

In this sort of entity, generally no members or owners are personally liable for activities of the LLC (that is, they have "limited liability"). In addition, if the LLC is classified as a partnership for tax purposes, when an asset is sold and money is distributed, unlike in a corporation there is only *one tax*, on the members or owners. All members or owners of an LLC can participate in management and still enjoy limited liability, which is not true for limited partners in a limited partnership.

Make sure your advisor understands all of the pros and cons of using an LLC and understands all of the state and federal tax rules and the organizational costs.

Although this is a new kind of creature and generally not tested in some states, a **limited liability company** may make sense for you. Check with your advisor. Make sure your advisor understands all of the pros and cons of using an LLC and understands all of the state and federal tax rules and the organizational costs. In addition, of course, all of the questions that are relevant when it comes to setting up a limited partnership to hold family property are relevant when it comes to setting up an LLC. Who is in charge? What happens if an owner wants to get out? What are people likely to disagree on in 5 or 10 or 20 years?

UNDIVIDED INTERESTS/TENANTS IN COMMON

Let's say John and Mary own Riverview and they don't want to set up a separate entity such as a partnership or an LLC. Instead, they give each of the children a 10% interest (known as an "**undivided interest**") in Riverview. Now John and Mary and the children are the owners of Riverview; they own Riverview as "**tenants in common**." Or, let's say that under John and Mary's wills, they leave Riverview to the three children equally. After the deaths of John and Mary, the three children will own Riverview as **tenants in common**, each with a one-third **undivided interest**.

When land is sold by **tenants in common**, each one pays tax on his or her share of the gain. Put another way, there is no "double tax," as in a corporation.

This is simple. This is easy. To set this up doesn't cost too much money or take lots of lawyers. But it could cost thousands and thousands of dollars in legal fees to fix.

There are at least two very serious planning problems that can arise when property is owned by **tenants in common**.

First, while each **tenant in common** has the right to use and enjoy the property, no decisions can be made about the use or disposition of the overall property *without the agreement of all the owners*. When John and Mary's three children own Riverview, if two of them want to sell to the highest bidder and the third does not, *nothing happens*. If two owners want to put a conservation easement on the property and the third does not, *nothing happens*.

Second, any **tenant in common** co-owner generally has the legal right to be "cashed out." John and Mary's daughter, Alice, could say to her co-owner siblings, "I'm not interested in Riverview. I'd like either one-third of the land, so I can sell it, or, since Riverview is worth $2,500,000, I'll sell you both my interest for $833,000 in cash." If the siblings don't want to cash out Sister Alice with either land or money,

Sister Alice can file a partition suit and go to court. The court can usually order the property divided up, *or the court can order that the property be sold and the proceeds split among the owners.* In addition, problems frequently arise among co-owners when it comes to the sharing of expenses and the sharing of use and benefits. In most cases there simply has been no agreement ahead of time how to work out these issues. With land values what they are today, co-ownership of a valuable piece of real estate has the potential to be enormously costly and enormously divisive and can make prudent planning for an important piece of property difficult if not impossible.

...co-own-ership of a valuable piece of real estate has the potential to be enormously costly and enormously divisive and can make prudent planning for an important piece of property difficult if not impossible.

TRUSTS

What about a **trust**? Again, let's start with a brief description. A trust exists

when someone holds assets for the benefit of someone else, or, put another way, when a trustee holds assets for the purpose of protecting or conserving those assets for beneficiaries. Like a corporation or a partnership, a trust may own assets. Unlike a corporation or partnership, however, a trust is not "owned" by anyone, although the beneficiaries are entitled to enjoy the assets according to the terms of the trust.

There are as many different kinds of trusts as there are lawyers who draft them and popular authors who advocate them. Some trusts are taxed like corporations and are subject to the "double tax" discussed above. Some trusts *could* be taxed like partnerships, that is, one tax, on the individual beneficiaries. Some trusts are taxed as *trusts*, which is a whole separate area of the tax code that is beyond the scope of this book. Some trusts are taxed *as if they didn't exist at all*, in other words, the "owner" of the trust, or the "grantor," is subject to tax on everything that happens in the trust.

Many landowners have been encouraged or advised to "put their land into a trust" *without any attention to tax consequences.* One extremely important word of caution. If you think you might want to use a trust as part of your family land planning, you must be absolutely certain that the lawyer you are working with understands the long-term planning consequences and *all* of the income tax and estate and gift tax consequences of what you are doing.

If you think you might want to use a trust as part of your family land planning, you must be absolutely certain that the lawyer you are working with understands... all of the... consequences of what you are doing.

One point of clarification. In some parts of the country confusion exists about "land trusts" and the sorts of trusts we discuss in this chapter. If you set up your own revocable or irrevocable trust (more on these below) for planning purposes, and deed your land into that trust, you *could* call that a "land trust" but attorneys would generally call it simply a "trust." In some parts of the country the term "land trust" refers to a situation when a trustee simply holds title to land on behalf of the real owner. For purposes of this book, however, as *Chapter 4* noted, a "land trust" is a tax-exempt charitable organization involved in land conservation and open space protection. If you give your land to a *tax-exempt land trust* you have actually *given your land away to a charitable organization*, and that is not the same thing as setting up a *trust of your own* for planning purposes.

THE MOST IMPORTANT THING TO REMEMBER ABOUT TRUSTS

I have heard too many people say, "Well, I put our land into a trust. Doesn't that take care of everything?"

No. It certainly *doesn't* resolve important questions about the future of your land. In addition, *just putting your land into a trust may not take care of any of your tax concerns, either.* It depends on what the tax consequences are of putting your land into *that type* of trust, and that depends generally on whether the trust is a "**revocable**" trust or an "**irrevocable**" trust.

REVOCABLE TRUSTS AND IRREVOCABLE TRUSTS

Revocable Trusts

Let's divide trusts into two different categories, revocable trusts and irrevocable trusts. And let's look at revocable trusts first.

A **revocable trust** is a trust you create that you can *revoke* at any time. In other words, you can *change your mind* at any time. You can rip up the trust instrument and make the trust go away; you can amend any or all of the provisions of the trust and completely change what's going on; you can *take out* of the trust any of the assets you have put into the trust. In effect, with a revocable trust, you may be using the trust to hold title to land or other assets, but you still retain complete control.

Because you still retain complete control, *for income tax purposes and for estate tax purposes* the tax law continues to treat you as the owner of all of the assets in the revocable trust. If you have stock in a revocable trust and the stock pays cash dividends, for income tax purposes you are treated as the owner of the stock and *you must pay tax on that income.* If you have land in a revocable trust and the land is sold, for income tax purposes you are treated as the seller of the land and *you must pay tax on the gain. And if you have land in a revocable trust and you die,* for estate tax purposes you are treated as the owner of the land and *that land is fully subject to estate tax in your estate.*

In many cases, there may be (and there are) perfectly good and legitimate reasons to put land or other assets into a revocable trust. If you become disabled or otherwise cannot manage your own affairs, a trust can provide for someone to see to centralized control and management of your assets. A trust may be a vehicle for avoiding probate (more on that below). A trust may otherwise be one part of a comprehensive estate plan or asset management plan.

But make no mistake about it. While there may be sound legal planning reasons for putting assets into a revocable trust, without taking additional planning steps there is *no tax benefit* from doing so. Without taking additional planning steps, *simply putting land into a revocable trust will be absolutely no help in lowering or avoiding estate tax.*

Avoiding Probate; "Living Trusts"

There is a great deal of popular literature encouraging people to put assets into trust to avoid probate. What does this mean? What doesn't it mean?

Put very simply, "probate" is the *process of estate administration as overseen by the probate court.* The will is filed in court, the court declares that it is genuine, a legal representative is appointed (often called the "executor"), papers are filed, assets are accounted for, estate tax returns are prepared when necessary, debts are paid. After federal and state estate tax audits are complete, distributions are made and the final accounting of the estate is filed with the probate court, as required by law. Because papers and accounts are filed in court, this part of "probate" is not a private process. By avoiding the probate court system, the process can be more streamlined, less public, and less expensive.

Again, put *very simply*, assets that pass to your heirs under the terms of your will ("I leave Riverview to the children") are subject to the probate process. Assets that do not pass to your heirs under the terms of your will are not subject to the probate process. The most common example of assets that are not subject to probate? John and Mary own Riverview jointly with right of survivorship. At John's death, Riverview passes *automatically* to Mary.

A "living trust" is simply a trust that you set up and transfer assets to during your lifetime. A "living trust" could be a revocable trust or it could be an irrevocable trust; generally, when this term is used in popular literature, it refers to a revocable trust. Assets that pass to your heirs under the terms of a revocable trust are not subject to probate. But pay careful attention. If John and Mary put Riverview into a revocable trust, and by the terms of that trust Riverview goes to the children after the deaths of John and Mary, the transfer of Riverview to the children will be automatic and will not be subject to the probate process. *But for estate tax purposes John and Mary are treated as the owners of Riverview and the value of Riverview absolutely will be subject to estate tax in their estates.*

> *...you should not be misled...into thinking that avoiding probate means avoiding estate tax. It does not!*

In many cases, for a variety of reasons, John and Mary may want to structure their affairs so some or all of their assets pass to the children through trusts or by some other manner that *avoids probate*. The reasons why they may or may not want to do this are complex, personal to John and Mary, and beyond the scope of this book. But John and Mary should not be misled, and you should not be misled, and millions of readers of popular bookstore literature should not be misled into thinking that *avoiding probate means avoiding estate tax. It does not!*

To get back to this chapter, *without taking specific additional planning steps there is no tax benefit to using a revocable trust.* To repeat, one more time: what are the *tax consequences* of using a revocable trust to "avoid probate"? *There may be none.* Using a trust for these purposes *may* be advisable (or may not), but *without additional planning* this sort of trust *won't even begin to address an estate tax problem.*

Irrevocable Trusts

When you put land (or other assets) into an **irrevocable trust**, as a general rule *you have given up control over that land.* You cannot rip up an **irrevocable trust** and make it go away. You *cannot change your mind* and take the land back out again. In addition, when you transfer land to an **irrevocable trust** *you may have to pay a gift tax;* remember the rule in Chapter 3 that, with exceptions, every transfer of wealth or value is potentially subject to gift tax or estate tax. However, using an **irrevocable trust** may have very favorable *long-term* tax consequences and may enable you and your heirs to avoid paying estate tax for one or more generations on the land in that trust.

A longer and more detailed discussion of irrevocable trusts is beyond the scope of this book. Check with your advisor for details.

In many cases today, family land has been "locked up" in a multi-generational trust that has solved some otherwise very difficult estate tax problems. But I am seeing an increasing number of situations in which the current trust beneficiaries disagree about what should happen to the land now, or are worried about what will happen to the land once the trust terminates. Mom and Pop (or Grandma and Grandpa) may have done some thoughtful and sophisticated *estate tax planning,* but as more and more beneficiary-owners come into the picture, generally with their hands tied, significant new problems arise. Solving these problems is at best a difficult job and is often simply not possible. On the other hand, keeping the property in the family for decades at a *relatively low tax cost* may turn out to be the tradeoff that a family wants.

However, it is certainly both fair and correct to say that while the terms of trust documents prepared many years ago are often inflexible, the trend in the law over recent decades has been toward increasing the flexibility of irrevocable trusts. If you think this may be an appropriate planning vehicle for you, a knowledgeable advisor can help you set up an **irrevocable trust** that can achieve both flexibility and long-term tax planning benefits.

Most of the time, when trust beneficiaries disagree about what to do with family land in an irrevocable trust, some beneficiaries want to sell for top dollar, some want to keep the land intact, and some are caught in the middle. Of course, the simplest way to avoid these sorts of disputes is for Mom and Pop to put a conservation easement on the land *before* they convey the land into the irrevocable trust. In fact, *this is a good general rule to keep in mind.* If you want to protect your land, and if you expect to use a trust or partnership or limited liability company ("LLC") to hold that land as part of the overall planning process, it may well make good sense for a variety of reasons to *put the conservation easement on the land before you convey it to an entity for the next planning steps.* For one

> *...it may well make good sense for a variety of reasons to put the conservation easement on the land before you convey it to an entity for the next planning steps.*

thing, the question of whether a trust, corporation, partnership, or LLC can make charitable contributions at all can raise complex legal issues. If you are the only owner, or if you and your spouse are the only owners, you don't need anyone else's agreement, or vote, or signature, to donate an easement.

Some More Things to Think About

If you are planning to put family land in a trust, you and your lawyer should also know the answers to these questions (among others). As with the earlier questions on page 49 in this chapter, the *issues* raised here may also be relevant if you use a partnership, S corporation, or LLC.

- ◆ Who are the beneficiaries? Are there ever going to be more beneficiaries?

- ◆ Who is the trustee (or trustees)? Is the trustee a bank or trust company? Can the beneficiaries remove and replace the trustees? Who can (or can't) be trustees?

- ◆ Are there gift tax consequences that arise from transferring land into the trust? What are they? What are the estate tax consequences to various generations of family members?

- ◆ Can you continue to use the land once it has been transferred to the trust? Can the children? Who decides? What are the tax consequences?

- ◆ Can you add more land or other assets to the trust in the future? If so, what are the tax consequences?

- ◆ Can the trustees distribute some or all of the land to the beneficiaries? If so, what are the tax consequences?

- ◆ What if the operation of the land costs money? What if the trust runs out of money? Can the trust charge rent? Must the trust charge rent?

- ◆ Can the trustees make charitable contributions from the assets in the trust?

- ◆ Can the trustees sell some or all of the land for development? Can the trustees sell some or all of the land to the beneficiaries? For how much? Can they sell the land at all?

♦ Are the assets of the trust protected from potential creditors of the beneficiaries?

♦ *What does the trust instrument say about what happens if in twenty or thirty years the trustees and the beneficiaries disagree about the answers to these questions?*

♦ Can the terms of the trust ever be changed?

CHARITABLE DEDUCTIONS

There is another potentially important difference among partnerships, corporations, and trusts when it comes to protecting the family's land. Remember the rule from *Chapter 4* that if John and Mary donate an easement on Riverview, they generally can take that deduction up to 30% of their income for the year. There is a five-year carryforward of any balance remaining from the deduction.

Remember that when a partnership sells an asset, the partnership pays no federal tax on any gain, but the partners pay tax. If the partnership owns Farmacres and donates an easement on Farmacres, the partnership does not take a deduction either. Instead, the partners take their individual shares of the deduction on their own tax returns. (In tax terms, the deduction "flows through" to the partners.) For example, if the easement deduction is $500,000,

Remember that when a partnership sells an asset, the partnership pays no federal tax on any gain, but the partners pay tax.

and if there are five equal partners, each partner can take a $100,000 charitable contribution deduction on *his or her own tax return* (subject to the 30%-of-income limitation).

If Family Corp. owns Farmacres and donates an easement worth $500,000, that deduction *can only be taken by Family Corp.* (not the shareholders) and that deduction *can only be taken up to 10% of Family Corp.'s taxable income for the year.* In most cases where family land is held in a corporation, and there is little or no income, the charitable contribution deduction for a conservation easement (or any other charitable deduction, for that matter) may very well be *"wasted" for income tax purposes.*

Obviously, if Family Corp. does in fact have significant taxable income, the income tax deduction from a charitable contribution can have significant tax benefits. Many very profitable corporations do in fact make charitable contributions and can and do deduct those contributions up to 10% of their entire taxable income. As is the rule with *individual* donations, any amount of a corporate charitable contribution not used in the first year can be carried forward by the corporation and used against corporate taxable income for five "carryforward" years.

If an S corporation makes a charitable contribution, as a *general rule* the deduction "flows through" to the S corporation shareholders just as a charitable contribution deduction by a partnership "flows through" to the partners. *But there are important limitations on the ability of shareholders to take deductions for charitable contributions by* **S corporations** *that do not apply to charitable contributions by* **partnerships**. The deduction of charitable contributions by a **trust** depends on how the trust itself is taxed.

In addition, as noted earlier in this chapter, the question of whether a trust, corporation, partnership, or LLC can make charitable contributions, and under what circumstances, can raise complex legal issues. Check with your advisor.

"I LEAVE MY STOCK TO MY CHILDREN..."

One further word about the various entities discussed in this chapter.

If you own **stock** in a **corporation**, that is a separate asset that is part of your estate when you die. You can give that stock away to your children while you are alive, or sell it, or leave it to them by will at your death.

The same thing is true about stock in an **S corporation**, or an interest in a **limited liability company**, or a **partnership interest**. Those are assets that *you* own. The corporation, or the LLC, or the partnership *owns the land* (or whatever else you may put into it).

If a **trust** owns land, and you are a **beneficiary** of that trust, the rules are different. As noted earlier in this chapter, a trust is not "owned" by anyone. Generally speaking, *the terms of the trust* control what happens in the future. Typically, if you set up a trust it might say, "the income from the trust is to be paid to our children for their lives, and at the death of the last surviving child the trust terminates and the assets in the trust are distributed to our grandchildren." Often, you cannot "give" your interest in a trust to anyone else (although sometimes you can). Sometimes you will not be subject to estate tax on the assets in a trust when you die, although *sometimes you will.*

TWO REMINDERS

First, this book is *an introduction* to some of these rules. The tax rules for partnerships, corporations, and trusts are complex. This chapter and this book are written in generalizations and only scratch the surface. You must consult with a competent tax advisor on all of these issues.

Second, many families around this country are now stuck with family land that was deeded into a corporation years or even decades ago. The corporate ownership, and the double tax the shareholders are facing, make planning incredibly more complicated and incredibly more costly. If someone tells you *today* to put your land in a corporation, please remember the advice at the beginning of this chapter.

WHAT HAPPENS IF:

What happens if the family:	Federal Tax on the sale of Farmacres?	Good for Estate Planning?	Favorable Treatment of Charitable Contributions?
Puts Farmacres in a limited partnership	One tax	Yes	Yes, but complex issues come up when lots of parties are involved
Puts Farmacres in a corporation	Two taxes	No	Possibly not for income tax benefits
Puts Farmacres in an S corporation	Possibly one tax; *possibly* two	Not bad; could do better	Possibly, although limitations apply and complex issues come up
Puts Farmacres in a limited liability company	One tax	Possibly	Yes, but complex issues can come up
Uses a revocable "living trust"	One tax	Absolutely not without more	Yes
Uses a "family trust"	Depends on the type of trust; maybe two taxes	Depends on the type of of trust	Depends on the type of trust
Uses outright ownership (undivided interests)	One tax	Could do better; could pose major problems	Yes, but all co-owners must agree

The chart above summarizes in very brief form what happens in some situations under various forms of ownership discussed in this chapter.

❦ 6 ❦
OTHER PLANNING TOOLS

MORE CHOICES

It may be that with no more than the planning tools we have covered so far, and with some hard work and hard thinking and communication, John and Mary, and Sue, and the Smith family, can make considerable progress in their own succession planning efforts. However, it's nice to have a larger menu of choices, and I'd like to cover four other planning possibilities in this chapter:

- life insurance;

- charitable remainder trusts;

- private foundations;

- gifts by will.

Please keep in mind that volumes (even small libraries) have been written about countless succession planning tools; again, this chapter and this book are intended to be *an introduction* to *some* of them. In addition, keep in mind, as I said in *Chapter 2*, that these are *established planning techniques* that should be on the menu of choices *whether or not* you own land. In the next few chapters, we'll see examples of how some of these techniques can be integrated with planning for your land so you can *protect your land, save on estate tax,* and *get more dollars to your children.*

LIFE INSURANCE

One of the most important and powerful long-term financial and estate planning tools available today is **life insurance**.

Historically, life insurance has had a lot of bad press. Today, a combination of creative planning techniques and favorable tax treatment of certain life insurance investments can be used to create a financial product that in many cases can do *more* than solve a family's land and tax problems.

Most People Do It This Way

First, let's look at the rather simple and conventional way life insurance is most frequently used. John wants to be sure Mary has financial security when he dies. John buys a $1,000,000 life insurance policy on his own life. John pays the premiums. At his death, Mary receives a check from the insurance company for $1,000,000.

Mary does not have to pay any estate tax (because of the **marital deduction**) on that $1,000,000. But when Mary dies, that $1,000,000 (assuming she still has it) is *subject to tax in her estate*. As we know, the children get a lot less than $1,000,000.

Or let's say that John is a widower, that Mary died first, and that their children are beneficiaries of the policy. At John's death, the $1,000,000 is to go to the children but that amount is *fully includable in John's estate* and is *all subject to estate tax*. As we know, the children get a lot less than $1,000,000.

For estate tax purposes, the general rule is simple. The proceeds of a life insurance policy are includable in the estate of the *owner of the policy*. The owner of the policy, generally speaking, is the person who owns or otherwise exercises control over the policy (for example, by being able to designate or change the named beneficiary or beneficiaries). When John dies, the proceeds of the policy *are includable in his estate*.

John Can Do Better Than That

Let's say that John sets up an **irrevocable trust** (recall the brief discussion of irrevocable trusts from *Chapter 5*). The irrevocable trust buys a $1,000,000 life insurance policy on John's life. John's children are the beneficiaries of the trust. Each year John contributes cash to the irrevocable trust, *and the trust uses that cash to pay the premiums on the life insurance policy.* At John's death *the proceeds of that life insurance policy will not be subject to tax in his estate. The full value of the $1,000,000 policy will be paid to the trust without estate tax.*

As usual in this book, it is important to emphasize that things can get a little more complicated, and that a number of other tax and planning considerations need to be taken into account. But the fundamental point is this: life insurance can be a very helpful planning tool.

One more important thing to understand about life insurance is that a policy on John's life alone may not be the most effective way to maximize the dollars that ultimately go to the children. It is possible to buy an insurance policy on the *lives of John and Mary* that pays the death benefit to the children (or to a trust for the children) on the death of the second spouse to die. This is often called a "**joint and survivor**" or "**second-to-die**" policy. By using the life expectancies of *two* people instead of just one, it is possible to buy *higher amounts of life insurance for generally the same cost.*

Second-to-die life insurance may give you tremendous "leverage" for your premium payments. However, if a surviving spouse expects to need additional income after the first spouse's death, second-to-die insurance *will not* take care of that planning problem, and a family will need to address that issue separately.

Professional advisors can disagree honestly about the wisdom of "investing" in a life insurance policy as opposed to the wisdom of "investing" the same dollars elsewhere. I believe it is important to emphasize that life insurance can be one of a number of *financial planning products* and should be considered as *on the menu,* among the range of many planning options available. Not only that, but in many cases people buy life insurance not only as a financial planning product but also *in case they die* (fancy that!).

You must be knowledgeable about the financial soundness of any life insurance company you work with; company financial statements and balance sheets and published credit ratings should be carefully scrutinized. If you are considering particularly large amounts of life insurance as part of the planning process, it may pay to diversify and buy policies from more than one company.

A good life insurance planner should be able to answer all of your questions and should be able to supply you with all of the information you need to help you through this part of the process, including information about the comparative stability of the various insurance companies. Remember, however, that even the best life insurance specialist is not likely to be a *tax* professional. You must work with an experienced tax attorney or a sophisticated accountant in connection with structuring and carrying out these transactions and in funding and working with life insurance trusts.

If you have a tax advisor you think you may be comfortable with, don't hesitate to ask questions. Of course, these are useful questions to ask your lawyer about *any* matter he or she may be working on for you.

Has he or she done this sort of work before? How many times?

What are some of the traps the advisor thinks you should avoid?

What other creative possibilities can the advisor offer?

What references can the advisor give you?

What will this cost you?

Finally, remember that in addition to your health, your *age* is a critical factor in determining the cost of life insurance. In other words, if you are interested, and if this planning tool makes sense for you, don't put it off for too long. The older you are, the more you will have to pay for life insurance. Even so, sometimes more life insurance is desirable for people of relatively advanced age.

THE CHARITABLE REMAINDER TRUST

Remember we said in *Chapter 5* that a trust exists when someone holds assets for the benefit of someone else. A **charitable remainder trust** is a particular kind of trust that when used properly can accomplish a number of important planning objectives. Setting up and using a charitable remainder trust can (1) generate an income tax deduction; (2) avoid capital gains tax on the sale of assets that have increased in value ("appreciated assets"); (3) increase your annual income; (4) serve as an important step toward further estate planning and financial planning for the family; and (5) help accomplish some of your charitable goals.

In one of its simplest forms, a charitable remainder trust (or "CRT") works this way. John and Mary transfer to the charitable remainder trust stock that has increased in value since they acquired it. John and Mary are entitled to an *income tax deduction*, based on the value of the stock they contributed and on actuarial factors from tables published by the IRS. The charitable remainder trust sells the stock and *pays no capital gains tax* because the CRT is treated as tax-exempt. (The charitable remainder trust would be likely to sell the stock through a stockbroker in the same way that John and Mary would have sold the stock if they had continued to own it themselves.) The charitable remainder trust then pays out income annually to John and Mary, for their lives. At the death of the survivor of the two of them, the charitable remainder trust terminates and pays the principal remaining in the trust to one or more charities.

Let's look at the important steps, and the results of the important steps, in a bit more detail.

Generating Income or Increasing Income

Let's say John and Mary have (among other assets) a $750,000 portfolio of stock that has increased significantly in value since John and Mary acquired it. Much of the stock has a low yield or no yield, and the annual rate of return on the portfolio is 2% (that is, $15,000 a year income to John and Mary). John and Mary would like a higher return from the portfolio, but in order to do that they would have to sell some of the highly appreciated stock and if they did that they would have to pay a large capital gains tax. It's just not worth it to them to do it this way.

If instead they transfer the stock to a CRT, the trust can sell the stock *without paying any tax.* John and Mary can be the trustees of the CRT and can determine how they want the proceeds of the stock sale to be invested (or they can hire an individual or a company to manage the investments for the CRT). Once the proceeds are reinvested, the trust can pay out a higher rate of income, for example 6%, and that means income to John and Mary of $45,000 a year. Although these particular taxation rules are complex, generally payments *from* the charitable remainder trust *will be taxable income* to John and Mary.

> *John and Mary can be the trustees of the CRT and can determine how they want the proceeds of the stock sale to be invested.*

Similarly, if John and Mary took highly appreciated land they were planning to sell and contributed that land to the trust, the trust could sell the land, *pay no tax on the gain*, reinvest *all* of the proceeds from the sale, and pay out a stream of income to John and Mary. Again, the periodic payments would be taxable income to John and Mary; again, at the death of the survivor, the money in the CRT is paid to charity. As another example, if John and Mary were not planning to leave their land to their children, but wanted to be certain it was protected, they could first put a conservation easement on it *then* contribute the land to a CRT; the CRT could then sell the land, pay no tax, and pay out income to John and Mary.

The charitable remainder trust rules are quite specific about the amount of income that must be paid out each year and how that amount is to be determined. Nevertheless, working within those rules, you can build in quite a bit of flexibility. Consult with your advisors for details. In addition, there are other charitable gifting techniques you may want to discuss with your advisors that involve combining a charitable gift with gifts to family members. For example, a **charitable lead trust** pays income to charity for a period of years, and at the end of the term of the trust the principal in the trust can go to family members.

A VEHICLE FOR FURTHER PLANNING — THE WEALTH REPLACEMENT TRUST

Now, if you're in the same sort of position as John and Mary, there may be a number of appealing points about a CRT. But if you're in the same sort of position as John and Mary's children, you might say, "Well, you know, this is nice for Mom and Dad, because they can use that additional income, but what about the $750,000 in the CRT *that was going to come to us?*"

Two points. First of all, if John and Mary hadn't set up the CRT, the $750,000 would have been fully subject to estate tax, so the three of you children might have divided up roughly $375,000, not $750,000.

Second, however, with that first qualification, the question does make a point. The price John and Mary had to pay in order to increase their annual income is that the money left in the CRT at the death of the survivor goes to charity.

Let's look again at life insurance.

Life insurance in an **irrevocable trust**, by itself and without further planning, can accomplish a number of important objectives.

A **charitable remainder trust**, by itself and without further planning, can accomplish a number of important objectives.

Many planners today, however, often suggest using the two "together." Here is how that would work.

Based on current prices in today's market, John and Mary can arrange to buy a $400,000 second-to-die life insurance policy for nine annual premiums of roughly $16,000 a year. If John and Mary also set up that charitable remainder trust with a 6% annual payment, for example, they will receive an annual income of $45,000 from the CRT until the death of the second spouse to die. Of course, for the first nine years (the period over which the life insurance premium payments are due), that additional $45,000 income from the CRT will help cover their annual payment of cash to the irrevocable trust (which will pay the life insurance premiums). Looking at *these assets alone*, the children can expect to receive $400,000 from the life insurance trust (free of estate tax) instead of closer to $375,000 as the after-estate-tax proceeds from the stock portfolio. In addition, of course, after John and Mary have died the principal remaining in the CRT will go to charity.

Using these two entities together creates what is often referred to as a **"wealth replacement plan,"** and it is obvious why that is so. And, used in this fashion (funded in effect by income payments from a charitable remainder trust), the life insurance trust is often referred to as a **"wealth replacement trust"** or **"wealth preservation trust."** The assets that could have been subject to estate tax were placed in the CRT and were "replaced" by life insurance proceeds that are free from estate tax.

PRIVATE CHARITABLE FOUNDATIONS

As noted in *Chapter 4*, as a general rule tax-exempt charitable organizations fall into two different categories. One type, that receives a broad base of financial support from many individual donors, is generally classified under tax rules as a **"publicly-supported"** charity and must meet certain tax law requirements to reach and maintain that status. A **private foundation** is your own personal charity, that is, a tax-exempt trust (or corporation) that you create. The individual, or family, or corporation creating the foundation may control its activities through the appointment of trustees or directors. In order to qualify for this tax exemption, the foundation must be created to support or conduct charitable and educational activities, such as the conservation and preservation of significant natural resources. (Sometimes the tax terminology can be a bit confusing. Many charitable organizations that use the word "Foundation" in their names are actually classified for tax purposes as "publicly-supported.")

Although a **private foundation** will not be a useful planning tool for most families, for other families a very important part of the overall planning could involve setting up a private foundation, providing it with funds to carry out charitable activities, and leaving land, cash, stock, or other assets to the foundation by will. (Remember from page 38 that a private foundation should *not* be the donee of a conservation easement.)

Because of perceived abuses in the private foundation area, often having to do with lavish spending of private foundation funds for the benefit of foundation donors, trustees, or managers, Congress in 1969 enacted a series of rules governing private foundations. Foundations generally must pay out most or all of their investment income, are subject to certain excise taxes, and are strictly prohibited from so-called "self-dealing" transactions, that is, transactions between a foundation and its principal donor or donors (and certain of their family members), trustees, and managers. The private foundation rules will restrict those who might abuse this important opportunity and will generally not be a problem at all for individuals or families who want to take advantage of the benefits a private foundation can offer for legitimate charitable purposes.

Anyone Can Do It

Any individual or family is free to start a private foundation and to use that foundation to further important charitable endeavors. Private foundations typically make grants out of their investment income to "public" charities; some private foundations fund or carry out their own charitable activities; some private foundations can acquire and hold important conservation land (but not easements), or historic property, for conservation or preservation purposes. Private foundations can be well-known and control enormous amounts of money; there are many with assets in excess of hundreds of millions of dollars. Private foundations can be more modest, be low-key, and make small but important grants each year to carry out the donor's chosen objectives. (In many cases, using an existing "community foundation" can be an alternative to setting up your own private foundation. Discuss this matter with your advisor.)

Tax Benefits

A private foundation can be established during the donor's lifetime or by will. Contributions to a private foundation during lifetime are deductible, although the contributions are subject to a set of charitable deduction limitation rules that are different from and generally less generous than the rules on contributions to public charities. Gifts left by will to a private foundation are *not subject to estate tax*; the estate tax treatment is the same as for gifts by will to public charities.

GIFTS BY WILL

A charitable gift of land, or a gift of a conservation easement, or a gift of cash to your *alma mater* or the local land trust, can be made during your lifetime, of course, and can also be *included in your will*, to take effect at your death. If you make a charitable gift by will, there will be no *income tax deduction* on your *income tax return*.

For estate tax purposes, the full value of the gift is included in your estate and then deducted from the estate. As a *tax* matter, it is as if the property had been restricted or given away before death, and kept out of the estate at the outset. Before you do this sort of planning, you should have an experienced estate-tax counselor make a careful analysis of the planning issues concerning a sizable charitable contribution left by will.

"When would I want to do that?" you might ask.

Gift of Land By Will

Most people simply will not want to *give away* land to a charitable organization, either during lifetime or at death. But in an increasing number of cases, landowners are revising their wills to leave important conservation land to charitable conservation organizations. In some cases, a landowner may not have close family heirs. In some cases, a landowner may care deeply about both protecting the land and making it available for others to enjoy. In some cases, a landowner may want to create a nature preserve, or protect an important habitat, and may believe that after his or her death a charitable conservation organization may be the best owner for those purposes.

In some cases, an important piece of family land may have become so valuable that even with the most creative estate-tax and conservation planning, the land, along with other family assets, will trigger an *enormous* estate tax bill, and the family may decide that giving the land away (by will) serves a strong conservation desire, provides significant estate tax relief, and "frees up" other assets for the heirs.

One word of caution if you care about your land and are thinking about giving your land away, either during your lifetime or at death. **Never trust an unrestricted piece of land**. Promises, handshakes, and understandings between you and the donee organization that your land will always be preserved and will never be sold for development *are not enforceable.* Times change, budgets change, boards change, and what you and a conservation organization believe today is important conservation land may one day after you're gone be looked on as a source of funds or as ideally suited for some other purpose than the one you had in mind.

If you want to give away your land and want to make sure it stays protected, please keep this in mind. There are some very technical tax reasons why you generally *should not* make a *gift of land* and include *restrictions in the same deed*. The IRS takes the position that if you do it this way your charitable deduction will be limited to the *restricted value of the land* (which may be significantly lower than the unrestricted value).

Here is one good way to be sure your land stays protected *and* that you can achieve the maximum tax benefits. *First* put a conservation easement on your land and give the easement to one charitable organization. *Then* give the land, restricted, to another charitable organization. If you do it this way, the charitable recipient of the gift of land can keep it or *can sell it, subject to the restrictions*, but the land will *remain protected.*

Gift of an Easement by Will

Let's look at a few situations in which a charitable conservation gift of an easement by will could be a very important planning device.

Donna, who is 82, has decided to put an easement on Mountain View Farm. She wants to see the farm protected, and she knows that the easement will bring significant estate tax relief. She has also decided to reserve three more house lots on the property.

Because of local ordinances, Donna will have to go through the town's subdivision process to secure approval for those additional building lots. She is willing to do that, but with surveys and engineering and meetings, it will be many months before the approvals are granted.

Because of her advancing age, and because she knows for sure that she wants Mountain View Farm protected (and wants her estate planning problems resolved), Donna decides to add to her will an easement on Mountain View Farm, *just in case* something should happen to her before the planning process has been completed.

Or take George and Martha, in their early fifties. George and Martha own Greenacres, a very beautiful and very valuable country estate with a large historic home and outbuildings. They inherited Greenacres from Martha's mother, who told Martha before her death to be sure to take proper care of Greenacres, and to see to it that the animals and flowers and trees were not disturbed. Martha's mother also left considerable money in trust for Martha and Martha's children. George and Martha are quite successful and fairly comfortable, and they know their children will be comfortable, too.

Because George and Martha do not yet know what the long-term financial future might bring, they are just a bit hesitant to restrict Greenacres with a conservation easement and give up the substantial value doing that would entail, although they think they may be willing to do that within the next few years. But George and Martha travel a lot, and they know that if anything happens to them Greenacres will pose a significant burden for their estate and will likely be sold, bulldozed, and developed.

George and Martha decide to add to their wills an easement on Greenacres. They will think about actually completing that gift in a few years, but in the meantime they have solved a few potentially difficult problems.

Things to Remember

If you do decide that an easement in your will is a prudent and desirable planning step, you should keep a few points in mind.

First, the text of the easement document should be worked out *in detail* with the potential donee organization, along with any possible endowment agreement, before the easement actually becomes part of your estate planning documents. You do not want to create a situation in which an unexpected easement gift will not be accepted or cannot be completed satisfactorily.

Second, language should be included allowing your executor to take appropriate steps, such as having survey work done, for example, or securing municipal approvals, if necessary, to complete the transaction.

Third, remember, just as with any other part of your will, *you can change your mind about an easement in your will at any time.* Should your thinking change, you can modify the easement in your will, eliminate the easement from your will, or, of course, you can go ahead and complete the easement gift while you are alive. Remember in this regard that your will controls what happens to property *you own in your own name when you die.* If George and Martha add to their wills an easement on Greenacres, but then convey Greenacres to a trust, or to a partnership, or to their children, *Greenacres can no longer be affected by the provisions of their wills.*

Tax Benefits

When you make a charitable gift by will, you are not subject to any of the percentage-of-income limitations (discussed in *Chapter 4*) that apply to income tax deductions for lifetime charitable gifts. Unlike a lifetime gift, which for income tax purposes is generally subject to a deduction ceiling of 30% of income, a gift by will is fully deductible for estate tax purposes.

Of course, any lifetime income tax savings are not available if you make a gift by will. If you are thinking about a charitable gift by will, you should also consider whether to complete that gift during your lifetime instead, to be able to take advantage of both the income tax benefits that will be available and the satisfaction of seeing the gift completed while you are alive.

✿ 7 ✿
SUE AND DIAMOND RANCH

THE FACTS

Now that we have learned some of the basic rules, let's see how we can apply them to help Sue and Diamond Ranch.

Let's review Sue's situation. As we learned in *Chapter 1*, Sue owns Diamond Ranch, worth $1,700,000, and she has $150,000 in other assets. The total estate tax due at her death is $520,500.

Sue and her two children agree they would like to see Diamond Ranch remain in ranching and agricultural use. They also agree that neither of the children expects to move back to Diamond Ranch after Sue's death.

AN EASEMENT

The first step in Sue's planning appears to be to determine the appropriate terms for a **conservation easement** on Diamond Ranch. Because of the important conservation values of Diamond Ranch, including the scenic views across the ranch, the important open space in an increasingly urban area, and the productive agricultural land, it seems clear that an easement would meet at least one of the "conservation purposes" tests. The easement could permit continued ranching and agricultural use but generally prohibit other commercial or industrial uses or residential development. If Sue followed this approach, such an easement would reduce the value of Diamond Ranch to $675,000.

However, let's also assume that Sue would like to preserve some additional value for her children, and she decides to reserve the right to create three additional house lots under the terms of the easement. Assume that easement reduces the value of Diamond Ranch to $900,000. Because Sue has lowered the value of Diamond Ranch, she has lowered the value of her entire estate to $1,050,000 (Diamond Ranch at $900,000 and $150,000 in other assets). *The total estate tax bill drops to $173,500.*

In addition, Sue is entitled to a large income tax deduction; recall from *Chapter 4* that Sue's total income tax savings from the deduction is $13,440. Finally, remember that the deduction from the donation "carries forward" for five years after the year of the gift.

WITHOUT THE DONATION

Year 1

Income: $40,000

Tax Due: **$6,246**

WITH THE DONATION

Year 1

Income: $40,000

Deduction: $12,000

Tax Due: $4,006

Income Tax Savings (over six years): $13,440

If Sue did nothing else, Diamond Ranch would be saved and it could be sold, and the house lots could be sold, subject to the easement. Even after payment of the state and federal estate taxes, her children would divide a substantial inheritance.

Note three things:

First, and this is very important, as suggested in *Chapter 4* Sue could donate an easement on a portion of Diamond Ranch, carry forward the deduction, then donate another easement on the balance of Diamond Ranch. The total income tax benefits could be greater this way.

Second, and this is very important, without doing any planning other than a conservation easement with some reserved house lots, Sue has solved the estate tax problem that would have forced the sale of Diamond Ranch for development. There are countless landowners all across the country who can do exactly the same thing: solve the estate tax problem with a conservation easement. In many of those cases, by using a conservation easement those landowners can reduce the value of the estate below $600,000 (or below $1,200,000 for a married couple with appropriate wills and planning), so that *no estate tax is due at all.*

Third, and this is very important, in the case of those landowners like Sue, who with a conservation easement can avoid the forced sale of family property to pay the estate tax, *there is more planning that can be done to save additional estate tax dollars.*

ANNUAL GIFTS

Recall in *Chapter 3* we discussed the "**annual exclusion**" that allows each person to give away $10,000 each year to as many people as he or she would like. Sue is unwilling to make large cash gifts to her children and grandchildren each year, but she certainly can use her **annual exclusion** *to give them interests in Diamond Ranch.* In fact, there are *at least* two different ways she could proceed.

First, Sue could decide simply to give her children, their spouses, and her grandchildren interests in Diamond Ranch; Sue could give them "**undivided interests**" and they all would be "**tenants in common**". Let's say that Sue wants to give each other family member up to $10,000 a year in value in Diamond Ranch under the annual exclusion rules. With Diamond Ranch worth $900,000 (subject to an easement reserving three additional house lots), a $10,000 interest in Diamond Ranch is roughly a 1.11% interest; Sue would need to execute deeds to each family member giving them a 1.11% interest in Diamond Ranch. With two children, their two spouses, and four grandchildren Sue *could* give away $80,000 worth of Diamond Ranch this year and next year for as long as she wanted to.

The estate tax savings could be substantial. If Sue takes full advantage of this planning opportunity, after three years, for example, she will have reduced her total estate by $240,000, from $1,050,000 (Diamond Ranch plus her other assets) to $810,000. In most states, the combined federal and state estate tax on that estate is $78,900, compared to $173,500 before she began her program of making annual gifts *and $520,500 before she even put the easement on Diamond Ranch!* After two more years of annual gifts, she will have reduced her total estate to $650,000 and the estate tax would be $18,500!

> *...landowners all across the country...can... solve the estate tax problem with a conservation easement. In many of those cases...no estate tax is due at all.*

However, recall also the discussion in *Chapter 5* that **tenants in common** have *equal rights,* can *ask to be cashed out,* can *file a partition suit,* etc. Although the risk of dissension and discord may appear to be small in the case of Sue's family she may decide that for a variety of reasons she would prefer to work out the terms of a family **limited partnership**. The partnership agreement will establish a management arrangement and will include appropriate restrictions on the ability of partners to transfer their ownership interests in the partnership and limitations on the ability of the limited partners to run the business of the partnership. Sue can use the partnership to begin giving away value. (Keep in mind that, as we discussed in *Chapter 5*, Sue could also choose to use a **limited liability company**. Without exploring all of the pros and cons, to keep things simple assume that Sue decides to use a partnership.)

Once Sue has established the **limited partnership** she can deed most or all of Diamond Ranch to the **limited partnership** *after she has restricted the property with a conservation easement.* (Recall the discussion on page 59 about why Sue should donate the easement before she deeds the land to the partnership.) Sue could be the general partner, which generally means she would control the business of the partnership. As we have discussed, she could begin giving away limited partnership interests each year to her children, possibly their spouses, and possibly her grandchildren.

SOME OTHER POSSIBILITIES

Remember that we started this chapter with at least one important assumption, that Sue and her family *wanted to see Diamond Ranch protected.* Protecting Diamond Ranch with a conservation easement will result in a lower estate tax but it will also result in less *dollar value* going to Sue's heirs. If Diamond Ranch is staying in the family, this is often an easy tradeoff. Even if Diamond Ranch is not staying in the family, for some families this is a tradeoff they are willing to make. If Sue's family decides that protecting Diamond Ranch is no longer important, the donation of a conservation easement gets taken off the planning list.

Even without a conservation easement, of course, Sue could make annual gifts of interests in Diamond Ranch (or of interests in a partnership that owned Diamond Ranch), and over time that could lower her estate tax bill significantly. Whether or not Sue used a conservation easement, and even whether or not Sue owned land that was suitable for a conservation easement, it *might make sense* for Sue to make *annual gifts to children and grandchildren in order to get value out of her estate.*

Assuming Sue still wanted to use a conservation easement as part of her planning for Diamond Ranch, Sue could decide that rather than putting most or all of Diamond Ranch into a partnership she could simply begin giving her family interests in one or more of the additional house lots permitted by the easement. Or, Sue could establish an **irrevocable trust** and begin giving **undivided interests** in Diamond Ranch to that trust. Sue also could consider the possibility of buying **life insurance**; the planning process could continue even further.

Sue understands that if she does no planning at all there will be a large estate tax and very little opportunity to keep Diamond Ranch intact. If that is not what Sue wants, Sue needs to understand that a conservation easement on Diamond Ranch is a very important planning tool.

Certainly, too, after thinking about this problem, and after thinking about the planning rules, Sue and her family may come up with other choices entirely. The point is that Sue understands *the cost of doing nothing.* Sue understands that if she does *no planning at all* there will be a large estate tax and very little opportunity to keep Diamond Ranch intact. *If that is not what Sue wants,* Sue needs to understand that a conservation easement on Diamond Ranch is a very important

planning tool. Further, Sue needs to understand that *taking additional planning steps* can save significant additional estate tax dollars.

Finally, recall the comment at the very end of *Chapter 5*: this book is an introduction to these rules and these rules are complex. Sue must consult with a competent tax advisor on all of these issues, and Sue and her advisor must **run the numbers**.

DISCOUNTS

Before we look at similar planning opportunities for John and Mary and Riverview, there is one other planning concept to cover. Let me illustrate that concept with an example.

Let's say that Diamond Ranch is worth $1,700,000 unrestricted and that ten members of Sue's family own Diamond Ranch equally, that is, each one owns a 10% interest in Diamond Ranch. What is the value of a 10% interest in Diamond Ranch? Is it $170,000? Would you pay someone $170,000 for one of those 10% interests so that you could be a co-owner of Diamond Ranch with nine members of Sue's family? Probably not, especially since you would have no real say in what happens to Diamond Ranch and if the opportunity to resell your interest for $170,000 was in fact very limited (do you know anyone else who might buy a 10% interest in Diamond Ranch for $170,000?).

Let's change the facts just a little and assume that Diamond Ranch is owned by the Diamond Ranch Limited Partnership, which has ten partners. What would you pay for a 10% limited partnership interest? Again, certainly less than $170,000.

The IRS and the courts have come to recognize that the value of such ownership can actually be *less than* a comparable percentage of the value of the property.

Because a "minority" owner in property or in a partnership generally

...because... ownership interest is not easily marketable, the courts have been allowing reductions in the value of such partnership interests...

has little or no say in management and because that ownership interest is not easily marketable, the courts have been allowing reductions in the value of such partnership interests *generally* in a range of ten percent to thirty-five percent. (This is an inexact science, and there is no absolutely clear answer to the question, "How much?" You should discuss this matter with your advisor and a professional appraiser.)

Let's see how this works in practice. Let's assume that Sue puts a conservation easement on Diamond Ranch, reserving three house lots. Let's assume that Sue sets up a limited partnership and deeds Diamond Ranch into the partnership, and that Diamond Ranch is worth $900,000. Remember that without any discount, a 1.11% interest in the partnership was worth $10,000. But if we assume that the value of a minority limited partnership interest in the Diamond Ranch Limited Partnership can be discounted by 25%, *with* a discount a 1.48% limited partnership interest is worth $10,000! This is because 1.48% of $900,000 is $13,320; $13,320 *discounted by 25%* is slightly less than $10,000.

Sue can protect Diamond Ranch, reduce her estate tax, and preserve her assets for her children and her grandchildren.

Using a discount, then, if Sue makes annual gifts of limited partnership interests to her two children, their spouses, and her four grandchildren for three years, she will reduce the value of her estate to $720,320. In most states, the combined federal and state estate tax on that estate is $44,518, again *compared to $520,500 before Sue began the planning.*

Clearly, this may be a way for Sue to move *additional value* out of her estate. However, the law is continuing to evolve as far as when and for what amount discounts are appropriate, so you must make certain your advisor is knowledgeable about these issues.

THE PLANNING PROCESS COULD CONTINUE

As we understand now, there are a number of other things Sue *could* do. She *could* establish an **irrevocable trust** and purchase **life insurance**. She *could* set up a **charitable remainder trust**, or CRT, contribute the three reserved house lots to the CRT, and use the CRT to sell those lots to avoid tax on the gain. Sue and her advisors should **run the numbers** to see specifically how the costs and the opportunities work out. Or Sue *could* stop here.

As long as Sue and her children and her advisors understand the planning options and the planning process, Sue can protect Diamond Ranch, reduce her estate tax, and preserve her assets for her children and her grandchildren.

WHAT HAPPENS IF:

What happens if Sue:	Estate Tax	What happens to Diamond Ranch?	Value of assets to family
Does nothing	$520,500	Sold for development	$1,329,500
Puts a conservation easement on Diamond Ranch reserving 3 house lots	$173,500	Sold but protected	$876,500
Puts a conservation easement on Diamond Ranch and makes annual gifts to family members for 3 years	$44,518; will be lower if Sue makes annual gifts for more than 3 years	Sold but protected	$1,005,482; will be higher if Sue makes annual gifts for more than 3 years (some tax due on sale; see #4 in Appendix)

The chart above summarizes *in very brief form* what happens to Diamond Ranch under some of the different possibilities discussed in this book.

DOING NOTHING

As the chart above illustrates, **doing nothing is a choice**, but if Sue and the family care about Diamond Ranch it may not be a very good choice.

☙ 8 ☙
JOHN AND MARY AND RIVERVIEW

WHAT DO JOHN AND MARY WANT?

At this point, we have enough information to understand that there are some *fundamental similarities* between Sue's situation and John and Mary's situation.

First, in both cases, the owners (and their families) care about the property they own, don't want to see that property paved over and bulldozed, and *face major federal and state estate tax bills.* In both cases, then, a conservation easement makes a great deal of sense.

Second, in both cases, the owners and their families understand that by making annual gifts of interests in their property, or interests in a partnership they set up to own their property, they can ease the orderly transition of that property, keep the property intact, and help lower the estate tax bill even more. Sue and John and Mary have enough information to get this far.

But the planning issues for John and Mary now start to get more complicated. At this point we have a good idea what the tax rules are but we don't yet know what the family wants.

Assuming John and Mary can solve the estate tax problem, do any of the children plan to live at Riverview in the future? In John and Mary's home or in another (as yet unbuilt) home? Do the children plan to sell Riverview in the future? Do they all agree on the future plans?

Do John and Mary plan to treat the three children equally? Are the three children married? Do *they* have children?

How are the children doing financially? Are they doing well? Poorly? What about their spouses? Will one of the children need significantly more (or less) help from John and Mary than the other two?

If John and Mary use a family limited partnership, who will be the general partner after their deaths? One child? More than one child?

There are no "right" or "wrong" answers to those questions or to the other planning questions included in *Chapter 5.* But in order to *do the planning right,* John and Mary, and their advisors, and their children, need to address these questions and, as best they can, need to answer them. *Putting a conservation easement on Riverview will preserve Riverview. Putting Riverview into a family limited partnership and making annual gifts of limited partnership interests to the children will lower the estate tax bill.* But **succession planning** for John and Mary, Riverview, and the children, and **tax, legal, and financial planning to get the family land to the children**, will involve a *planning process* that considers a whole range of issues for family members now and into the future. Let's look at *one potential possibility* of how that planning process might come out.

> ### John and Mary, and their advisors, and their children, need to address these questions...

JOHN AND MARY LIKE WHAT THEY HAVE LEARNED

When John and Mary left their lawyer's office in *Chapter 1,* they thought something was wrong. They were right.

Riverview was going to be lost. Whatever hopes John and Mary had of protecting their little piece of the world were not going to be fulfilled. Whatever plans one or more of the children might have had for keeping up the family traditions at Riverview were not going to be realized. Whatever possibilities might have been available to John and Mary to lower their estate tax burden were not going to be explored.

By the end of *Chapter 6*, we saw a number of the planning tools that are available for John and Mary, and the family, *and for Riverview*, and in *Chapter 7* we saw how Sue and her family could take advantage of some of those tools. Keep in mind that under John and Mary's "estate plan" in *Chapter 1*, the three children divided approximately $2,352,000, *not including Riverview*, which was sold out of the family for development. By using a conservation easement and perhaps a family partnership, with annual gifts to the children and grandchildren, John and Mary now know they can protect Riverview and save a significant amount of estate tax.

But John and Mary like what they have learned, and there is a comprehensive plan they want to consider. These are the steps. Remember that Riverview is worth $2,500,000 and that John and Mary have $1,500,000 in other assets.

A CONSERVATION EASEMENT

First, John and Mary put a **conservation easement** on Riverview, this time prohibiting any further development or subdivision. The value of Riverview, so restricted, is $1,000,000. The income tax savings from the deduction are roughly $18,000 a year for six years (see *Chapter 4*).

A PRIVATE FOUNDATION

Second, John and Mary establish the John G. and Mary M. Landowner Family Foundation, a **private foundation** with the board comprised of family members (and perhaps a trusted advisor). Although the Landowner Family Foundation is free to pursue a wide range of charitable causes, John and Mary and the children anticipate that it will make most of its grants to publicly-supported charities in the land conservation and animal welfare fields. John and Mary make an initial $100,000 cash contribution to the Foundation.

A CHARITABLE REMAINDER TRUST

John and Mary then establish a **charitable remainder trust**, and they contribute to the trust stock worth $750,000. Under the terms of the trust, John and Mary are to be paid 6% of the trust's value annually for their lives. The trust sells the stock and reinvests in higher-yield instruments. Under the terms of the **charitable remainder trust**, after the deaths of John and Mary the principal of the trust goes to the John G. and Mary M. Landowner Family Foundation. (Check with your advisor about the income-tax-deduction limitations that may apply to their gift of stock to the CRT.)

NEW WILLS WITH A VERY DIFFERENT RESULT

Next, John and Mary revise their wills. Under their new wills, they make maximum use of their **unified credits** ($600,000 each), so that $1,200,000 of assets, consisting of Riverview and sufficient cash to reach the $1,200,000 plateau, go directly to their elder daughter. At the death of the second spouse to die, *all of their other assets go directly to the Landowner Family Foundation. There is no estate tax*! The Foundation now can anticipate some day having more than $1,000,000 in assets, from the CRT and from the estate of John and Mary Landowner.

LIFE INSURANCE IN AN IRREVOCABLE TRUST

Finally, John and Mary establish an **irrevocable trust** and arrange for the trust to purchase a $2,000,000 second-to-die **life insurance** policy. The premiums are funded by annual cash payments to the trust from John and Mary, made in large part out of their increased cash flow from the CRT and the income tax savings from the charitable contribution of the easement. The trust is drafted to operate as a so-called generation-skipping trust.

Although they still have not completely solved the problem of dividing their assets equally among their three children, they decide that of the total $2,000,000 that will come to the trust at their deaths, $400,000 will be separately earmarked for their daughter who will own Riverview and her children, and $800,000 each will be earmarked for their other two children and their families. John and Mary and their daughter who will inherit Riverview have spent time specifically going over the numbers to be certain that the daughter who will inherit Riverview will be able to afford its annual maintenance and upkeep.

WHAT IS THE EFFECT OF ALL THESE STEPS?

The total value going to the children: **$3,200,000** *including Riverview, protected.*

The total value going to the family's private foundation, to help further their philanthropic interests: **more than $1,000,000**.

The total estate tax paid: **zero**.

Remember this. If John and Mary had done *no planning*, the total amount going to the children would have been **$2,352,000**. And Riverview would have been sold (and probably developed) to pay estate taxes.

THE ZERO ESTATE TAX PLAN

What are the elements of the "**zero estate tax**" plan?

First, either all assets must go to charity at death or, as in John and Mary's case, the family must make effective use of the **unified credit**. Second, (within limits) wealth given away to charity *can be replaced* with **life insurance**, with proper planning.

The **charitable remainder trust** is not necessary, although it may be helpful and useful. In many cases, where land that is expensive to maintain (or an easement) is going to a charitable organization by will, using a **charitable remainder trust** is one way to commit the "endowment" ahead of time.

93

A family **foundation** is not necessary, although it may be helpful and useful. For some, a private family foundation is an important way to institutionalize and perpetuate a family's pattern of charitable giving into future generations. For others, outright gifts or bequests to other existing charities may be as satisfying and simpler.

If you care about your land, a **conservation easement** is necessary. It's the best tool we have so far for ensuring that the conservation values of your land will always be protected.

WHAT HAPPENS IF:

What happens if John and Mary:	Estate Tax	What happens to Riverview?	Value of assets to family
Do nothing	$1,648,000	Sold for development	$2,352,000
Put a conservation easement on Riverview with no additional reserved house lots	$1,098,000	Riverview is protected but we need more information; further planning may be necessary	$1,902,000
Take all the steps discussed in Chapter 8	0	Protected; goes to their elder daughter	$3,200,000 (not including more than $1,000,000 to the family foundation)

The chart above summarizes *in very brief form* what happens to Riverview under some of the different possibilities discussed in this book.

DOING NOTHING

As the chart above illustrates, **doing nothing is a choice**, but if John and Mary and the family care about Riverview it may not be a very good choice.

⚘ 9 ⚘
THE SMITH FAMILY AND SANDY POINT

THE SMITH FAMILY NEEDS TO UNDERSTAND THE PROCESS

When it comes to succession planing for family lands, there seem to be two kinds of patterns that families fall into.

In the first kind of case, like Sue's family and like John and Mary, there is agreement, or at least agreement on at least two fundamentals, at the outset: the family wants to protect the land, and the family wants to reduce the estate tax bill.

In the second kind of case, like the Smith family, not only is there not yet agreement but the potential exists for serious, fundamental, and costly disagreement. Recall the facts, briefly. Sandy Point is owned by four **tenants in common**: Sarah, Patricia, Lucy's trust, and Tom's family corporation. Each **tenant in common** owns a 25% **undivided interest**. Sarah and Patricia use the property; Tom doesn't. Sarah could use cash. Patricia wants to keep Sandy Point just the way it is. Tom's views are not clear. The trustee of Lucy's trust wants to sell for top dollar. And Sandy Point is worth $5 million.

Many families today, like the Smith family, face some of these issues:

- ◆ the family owns a large and valuable piece of land, usually unrestricted (making fights over value more likely);

- ◆ the land is often in agricultural, ranching, hunting, family recreation, or forestry use (or some combination of these uses);

- ◆ the family relationships are not always good, although they are often not bad; the potential for volatility exists;

- the family often has an opportunity for intergenerational planning, that is, using some of the assets in the estate of the older generation to help the younger generations keep the property;

- the family has usually not done any planning work dealing with the property itself (appraisal, land use planning, etc.);

- often, the existing ownership structure is complicated and doesn't work very well;

- often, the existing ownership structure is not at all efficient or helpful for tax and legal planning purposes, sometimes because of prior advice given without regard to long-term ownership issues or tax consequences;

- perhaps most important, the family has almost no idea what the tax and legal options are.

The key to solving the problem for the Smith family, and other families like the Smith family, is to understand the process.

The key to solving the problem for the Smith family, and other families like the Smith family, is to understand the process. The advisor who understands the process and can walk the family through the process is going to be as much like a "consultant" as an attorney. The process involves much more than tax planning: the process involves *gathering information, understanding the tax and legal rules, regular communication between the advisor (or advisors) and the family, consensus building, and implementing the result.* As we learned in *Chapter 2*, as a general rule, the process can be broken down into more or less separate parts.

PART I: GATHERING AND ANALYZING INFORMATION

Broadly speaking, the first steps involve gathering information, analyzing the information and *the tax planning choices,* and applying the relevant tax rules. As part of this process, a range of some possible results may emerge and some possible results may be ruled out.

What are some of the things that the advisor and the family can do? What are some of the questions that need to be answered? What do the various family members really want? ***What are the family's goals?***

Does anyone want to keep Sandy Point?

Does anyone want to keep Sandy Point for future generations of family members?

Who wants to sell? For top dollar? For less than top dollar if another family member is buying? (Note that "value" is not always clear but "price" is negotiable.) For less than top dollar if the property is dedicated to charitable uses?

Does anyone want to see Sandy Point protected against development? Permit limited development only?

Does anyone want to see Sandy Point dedicated to charitable, environmental, and educational purposes? Are any of the family members willing to contribute money for that purpose?

Is anyone willing to buy out one or more of the other owners?

Do the owners understand the estate tax consequences of owning a 25% **undivided interest** in a $5 million piece of real estate?

If some of the owners retain ownership and others don't, after a "reorganization" who will be in control in the short term? In the long term?

What are the tax and financial situations of each owner? Can they use charitable deductions? What do they *need?* What do they *want?* Are they willing to compromise to get to a result that keeps the family out of a major and costly fight over the future of Sandy Point?

Do the owners all understand the **cost of doing nothing**?

What are the tax rules and what are the tax issues? In addition, since Sarah and Patricia own their interests individually, the tax consequences of *any* outcome are likely to be different for them than for the trust or for Tom's family's corporation.

What are the tax consequences to each owner if Sandy Point is sold? Given to a charitable organization? Restricted by an easement?

Are there creative tax planning opportunities for each owner to lower the tax cost of a sale? To increase the tax benefits from a charitable gift? To fund a buyout of one or more of the owners?

It will almost certainly be necessary to have at least one meeting of all interested family members to go over the issues and to go over the tax planning options in detail.

Can the trust make charitable contributions? Can the corporation?

What are the estate tax consequences of continued private ownership for each owner?

It will almost certainly be necessary to have at least one meeting of all interested family members to go over the issues and to go over the tax planning options in detail. There are other issues, too, that may require bringing together a team to advise the family.

What does the family need to know about state and local law? What are the local land use and zoning rules, and how do those rules impact the value of Sandy Point and the planning possibilities?

What is Sandy Point really worth?

What is Sandy Point really worth if there is going to be limited development?

If there is going to be limited development, where do the house lots go? How does the family retain value in the reserved house lots while at the same time protecting the habitat, protecting the scenic view, and generally protecting the conservation values of Sandy Point?

Will family members need a professional facilitator, a neutral, impartial party, to help keep the planning process on track?

Assimilating all of this information, learning what's possible, and what works, and at what cost, is the first phase of the process.

PART II: CONSENSUS BUILDING; TAX PLANNING

The second phase of this process involves moving toward the family's goals for Sandy Point through consensus building; this will be the heart of the early planning. Good tax planning is a critical part of this phase for all of the owners (and all of the family members). *Participants are better able to make informed choices if they have a clear understanding of the bottom line after-tax dollar results and possibly a present value analysis of various options, including the option of doing nothing.*

The purpose of this book is not to take the Smith family and Sandy Point through a hypothetical planning process to reach a hypothetical conclusion. The goal here is to share with you some of the fundamental rules and a view of *the planning process*. That having been said, however, let me list below, in no particular order of preference or priority, a few (but by no means all) of the possible outcomes for Sandy Point and the Smith family based on my own experience.

◆ Sandy Point could be sold.

- The family could put a conservation easement on Sandy Point, reserving a portion of the property for limited development. Those owners who insisted on being cashed out could be bought out from the development proceeds.

- Lucy could become involved in the planning so that some of her assets could be used to help finance the buyout of owners who want to get out.

- The family could set up a private foundation for environmental research and education, scientific research, and public education, and Sandy Point could be given to the foundation.

- Lucy could become involved in the planning so that some of her assets could help finance the foundation approach, potentially with very favorable estate planning results for Lucy (and her family).

- Lucy might die before the family figures out how to combine estate planning opportunities for Lucy with the planning for Sandy Point.

- Communication could break down among the family members, and they could all hire lawyers and sue each other over the future of Sandy Point.

Whatever the result, the goal of Part II of the planning process is to reach consensus.

PART III: IMPLEMENTATION

This phase of the process will include moving to and implementing the result, preparing all related documents, coordinating work among various family members and other advisors as necessary, etc. This may involve a reorganization with the same or some of the same participants, sales and/or buyouts, creation or use of one or more new entities, estate planning documents, etc.

PART IV: ESTATE PLANNING FOR THE FAMILY MEMBERS

Once the future direction of Sandy Point is generally clear, a complete review of estate planning issues for each of the family members should be undertaken. The resolution of the Sandy Point project will have a *direct and significant* impact on *estate planning problems* and *estate planning opportunities* for Tom, Sarah, Patricia, and potentially for Lucy.

We don't know what's going to happen with Sandy Point. But by now we understand the planning process and we understand a lot of the tax and legal rules. What would *you* do if you were Tom, or Lucy, or Sarah, or Patricia, or one of their attorneys?

WHAT HAPPENS IF:

What happens if the Smith family:	Tax Issues	What happens to Sandy Point?	Family Harmony?
Does nothing	Complicated; especially estate issues for Sarah and Patricia	Unclear, *probably* sold for development	Unclear; *probably* not good
Sells Sandy Point	Substantial tax to be paid; *good tax planning* is imperative	Developed	Unclear
Goes through the planning process	Satisfactorily addressed, we hope	Unclear, but *the family makes the decision*	Good, we hope

The chart above summarizes *in very brief form* what happens to the Smith family and Sandy Point under some of the different possibilities discussed in this book.

DOING NOTHING

As the chart on the previous page illustrates, **doing nothing is a choice**, but if the Smith family cares about Sandy Point it may not be a very good choice.

✿ 10 ✿
A FEW FINAL WORDS

Every family is different; every piece of land is different. Financial, personal, and emotional needs change just as land use and landscapes change.

Succession planning for family lands is a process. The family needs to understand the rules and the family needs to understand the process. Every step in the process has a benefit and a cost; the cost of doing nothing is particularly high.

Readers need to remember that from time to time Congress does change the tax code and from time to time the IRS changes its interpretation or administration of the tax code; check with your advisor to be certain you are current. Over a number of years, for example, Congress has considered changing the estate tax rules, including possibly raising the $600,000 unified credit amount to $750,000 or even $1,000,000. Congress may also consider various additional tax incentives for private land conservation efforts.

Would passage of any of these measures eliminate the need for doing the planning? Absolutely not! If anything, it seems to me, passage of additional tax code incentives for private land protection would present a wonderful opportunity to emphasize to landowners all across the country how important it is to do timely planning. A lower estate tax may save dollars now, and that is important, but it certainly doesn't solve the problem of what happens to Riverview when John and Mary die, or what happens to Diamond Ranch ten or twenty or thirty years from now, or how the Smith family can resolve the future of Sandy Point.

In other words, whether or not tax rules or tax rates change, the underlying message of this book will be the same: if you are a landowner, and if you love the land you own, you'd better do some planning.

To repeat, this book is an introduction to the planning process and to *some* of the tools. This book is not intended to be all-inclusive, or exhaustive, or to give to you all the "right" questions or the "right" answers. This book is intended to get you started in the planning process. There will be legitimate personal, tax, or financial reasons why some of these tools may not be appropriate in some cases, just as there will be other tools or approaches that may be ideally suited for other cases. But if you care about your land, *you cannot just do nothing.*

I hope this book is helpful.

Stephen J. Small
Boston, Massachusetts
March, 1997

✿ APPENDIX ✿
TEN OTHER THINGS YOU SHOULD KNOW

1. *Don't do the planning without understanding the tax consequences of the planning you're doing.*

Note the following observations. These observations are relevant whether your situation is relatively simple, such as Sue's, or quite complicated, like the Smith family.

First, some of the tax rules in the following areas are complex and poorly understood:

- ◆ the estate and gift tax rules on transfers between family members;

- ◆ the taxation of corporations, partnerships, limited liability companies, and various kinds of trusts;

- ◆ the tax rules on qualifying for charitable contribution deductions generally;

- ◆ the tax rules on qualifying for conservation easement deductions;

- ◆ the appraisal and valuation rules and requirements.

Second, you can lose significant tax benefits and tax savings by going through a planning process that doesn't take into consideration all of the relevant tax rules. I have seen countless projects where families could have taken advantage of tax benefits but the planning process was seriously flawed by the absence of a clear understanding of the rules and planning opportunities. Here is an example.

A family engaged local counsel and land planning consultants who designed a large-lot subdivision. Although the total number of houses under the plan is not high, the location of the houses throughout and across the property makes it impossible for the family to meet the "conservation purposes" test for a deductible conservation easement.

Third, poor planning can cost of hundreds of thousands of dollars in lost tax savings and can even create additional taxes.

One more example. A family hired land planning and appraisal consultants who prepared extensive reports, including an analysis of the tax cost of land sales and tax benefits from a conservation easement donation. The family continued planning based in part on the consultants' conclusions. Because of a complex ownership structure, including land ownership by a family corporation, and an incorrect assumption about complex tax rules, the consultants' conclusions were in part unrealistic and in part simply wrong. In this case, *neither the family nor the advisors understood what the rules were.*

It is important to consult *at the outset* with an experienced tax advisor. This consultation does not have to be a long involved process. But understanding the tax rules *at the outset* can set the stage for the rest of the planning to go forward *so that the maximum possible tax benefits can be available at the appropriate time.* Committing to this additional level of planning *at the beginning*, and making sure all of the advisors understand what the relevant tax rules are, can potentially save a significant amount of money at the end. If the process gets underway without an understanding of all of the relevant rules it may turn out to be impossible to go back and fix things at a later date.

How do you know if you have the right tax advisor? Remember the questions in *Chapter 6.*

Has he or she done this sort of work before? How many times?

What are some of the traps the advisor thinks you should avoid?

What other creative possibilities can the advisor offer?

What references can the advisor give you?

What will this cost?

The family doctor is not shy about referring matters to a specialist; patients often *expect* that. An attorney who may be the family's primary legal care provider should not be uneasy about bringing in a specialist who can help out in a specific area.

2. *Treating the children equally, or fairly?*

When it comes to estate planning, when it comes to dividing up the after-estate-tax assets, most parents believe they need to *treat their children equally*. Generally, of course, this is a reasonable place to begin the planning.

However, especially when an important piece of family land represents a significant amount of the value in the estate, and especially when not all of the children have an equal interest in living on, owning, or otherwise enjoying that land, it may be difficult if not impossible *to treat the children equally*. Many families have come to understand that their goal isn't to treat the children equally but their goal is *to treat the children fairly*. It may be necessary, as John and Mary found in *Chapter 8*, to give the child who inherits the land more total "dollar value" than the other children, while at the same time that heir receives *less cash*. Again, this is a situation that can vary dramatically from family to family, but the sooner the family understands what the issues are, and the sooner the family begins to communicate about these questions, the more likely it is that the family can agree on a *fair outcome*.

3. *Planning in an emergency: planning by will*

Recall I pointed out in *Chapter 6* that you can donate an easement by will. In fact, in some situations *planning by will* can have a dramatic impact.

In one particular situation I am familiar with, the landowner was a successful businessman who had done the usual comprehensive and sophisticated planning for his other assets *but not for his land*. He was diagnosed with a very aggressive cancer, his condition deteriorated rapidly, and the normal planning process was compressed into a very short period of time. Once the landowner and the family agreed on a plan for his important real estate, however, a new will was prepared.

Under the will, the landowner (1) left a portion of his property unrestricted; (2) put a conservation easement on a portion of his property; (3) set up a private foundation and named his children as trustees; and (4) left the balance of his property, which was the most environmentally significant part, to the private foundation.

The moral of the story? Don't wait; do the planning now. But don't forget that in an emergency situation *planning by will can be extraordinarily effective.*

4. The important tax concept of "basis", including "carryover basis" and "stepped up basis at death"; run the numbers.

The concept of "basis" is a tax law concept. In many (but not all) situations, for tax purposes "basis" and "cost" mean the same thing. This is a *very simple illustration*, but if you buy stock for $1,000, and sell it for $2,000, you pay tax on the $1,000 gain, which is the difference between what you sold it for and your basis of $1,000.

In some situations, again for tax law purposes, cost is not the same as basis. If you buy an office building for, say, $500,000, and take annual *depreciation deductions*, those depreciation deductions will *lower the basis of the building*.

Recall that John and Mary originally bought Riverview for $100,000. That was their basis. John and Mary made many improvements to Riverview over the years; some of the money they spent on those improvements can be *added to the basis of Riverview*, again, for tax purposes. To keep this illustration simple, we'll ignore those expenses and adjustments.

If John and Mary sell Riverview for $2,500,000, they pay tax on the gain of $2,400,000 (the difference between the selling price and the basis).

If John and Mary hold Riverview until they die, and then leave it to their children, the estate tax will be based on the $2,500,000 value of Riverview. However, when their children inherit Riverview it will have *a basis in their hands* of $2,500,000. The tax laws refer to this as a **"stepped up" basis** at death; that is, the basis is "stepped up" or increased to $2,500,000. If the children inherit Riverview and then sell it for $2,500,000, there will be no gain and no tax to pay on the sale (although remember there was an *estate tax* on John and Mary's estate).

If John and Mary *give* Riverview to their children while John and Mary are still alive, there will be a *gift tax* to pay (recall *Chapter 3*) and the *basis* of Riverview in the hands of the children will be the same as the very low basis in John and Mary's hands, *plus* a portion of any gift tax paid. In tax law terms, *when there is a gift the basis of the prior owner* **"carries over"** *to the new owner.*

If John and Mary give interests in Riverview to their children taking advantage of the annual exclusion, John and Mary's very low *basis* in those interests (which will be a proportionate part of John and Mary's basis in Riverview) will carry over to the children. Again, the basis "carries over" in the case of a gift.

In some cases, particularly when a family does not intend to keep a property, it *may* make sense for landowners in John and Mary's case *not* to make gifts of interests in their property because of the **carryover basis** rule. Rather, it may make sense to hold the property until death in order to take advantage of the **stepped up basis**, possibly even at the cost of paying some estate tax. In other cases, the planning opportunity to make a series of annual exclusion gifts to many younger-generation beneficiaries, even with the carryover basis result, will make more sense than not making gifts, possibly paying increased estate tax, and receiving the property with a stepped up basis.

How do you know which choice to make? **Run the numbers**. Sit down with a competent tax advisor and *compare the possibilities*, including the possibility of *doing nothing*. If you make annual gifts, what are the *bottom-line after-tax dollar results*? If you don't, *what are the results? Don't assume;* **run the numbers**.

5. *Check the title early.*

Under the tax rules for conservation easements, if there is a mortgage on your property you can't get an income tax deduction for donating a conservation easement unless the mortgage holder "subordinates" the mortgage to the terms of the conservation easement. That is, the mortgage lender must agree that a foreclosure of the mortgage will not wipe out the easement. In addition, as you will see next in this *Appendix*, if you don't own all the minerals associated with your land, you may not be able to get a deduction for a conservation easement unless you meet certain tax law requirements.

Especially in the case of landowners who have owned their property for decades, it is important to clarify that the ownership rights are exactly as the owner thinks they are. I have been involved in more than one case in which the owner *thought* that title to the property was clear and clean, and a title search revealed liens, prior conveyances of mineral interests, etc. While the matters raised by some of these title issues may certainly be solvable, it is better to know about some of these outstanding matters *early* in a transaction rather than *late* in the transaction. Especially if you are planning to make an easement donation near the end of the year and enjoy the income tax benefits of a charitable contribution in that year, it is certainly advisable to *examine the title as early in the transaction as possible*. This way, if there are any surprises, or if anything shows up on the record that needs to be dealt with, you will have plenty of time to do that.

6. *Mineral Rights*.

The tax rules say that if you don't own the minerals on your property you can't get a deduction for a conservation easement without satisfying specific conditions. In some parts of the country, such as New England and the mid-Atlantic states, this is generally not an issue, because most landowners also own the minerals under their property. In many western states, however, land use patterns have developed under which prior owners (including the federal government) are reasonably likely to have "severed" or "separated" mineral interests from the rest of the property. In a typical situation, the seller might have said, "Here's the deed to my ranch, but I reserve the right to all of the oil, gas, and other minerals on my property." The situation is also not uncommon in the southeast and in the far northwest, and I recently learned of a situation in a town in New York where the mineral interests had been separated in the 1700s.

The relevant part of the tax rules says generally that if you don't own the minerals, you can't get a deduction for donating a conservation easement *unless* (1) the minerals were first separated from the rest of the property prior to June 13, 1976, and (2) you can establish that the likelihood of surface mining on the property is "**so remote as to be negligible**."

This "**so remote as to be negligible**" test is a tax law term of art, but it can generally be satisfied with a geologist's report establishing either that there are no potentially valuable minerals on or near the property or that if there are it simply isn't worthwhile as an economic matter to extract them. The mineral interest rules are highly technical and an experienced advisor should be consulted about this issue.

Once again, the important nature of this rule simply emphasizes the need to check the title early.

7. *Easements or restrictions that don't meet the tax code rules.*

Throughout prior decades, owners of family businesses have engaged in a variety of sophisticated transactions to get those businesses through the estate and gift tax system to the next generation of owners. In many cases, owners of family businesses would impose restrictions on the transfer of stock of the business in order to lower the value of that stock for tax planning purposes. The IRS litigated a number of cases in this area, and contested the validity or effect of such restrictions, but often was not successful in challenging these plans.

In the late 1980s and early 1990s, Congress addressed this issue with so-called "estate freeze" legislation aimed at some of these devices that business owners were using. Now Section 2703 of the tax code says that for estate and gift tax purposes, restrictions on the use or transfer of an asset (with certain exceptions) *will be disregarded when it comes to valuing that asset.* Of course, read literally this rule would mean that if you put a conservation easement on a piece of property, and meet the tax code requirements for that conservation easement, the restrictions imposed by that conservation easement will be disregarded for valuation purposes. This was certainly not what Congress intended, and the IRS regulations under Section 2703 acknowledged that by simply saying that the restrictions *will* be taken into account if you have donated a *qualifying* conservation easement. Of course, the law should have made that clear in the first place.

However, what is implicit in the rule of Section 2703 and the regulations is that if you have a restriction that *did not* meet the tax code requirements for conservation easements, *that restriction may be ignored for valuation purposes.* Put another way, as one example, if instead of a *perpetual* restriction you have a *thirty-year* restriction on your property, limiting or prohibiting its development for thirty years, what Section 2703 seems to say is that *the thirty-year restriction will be ignored in valuing that property for estate and gift tax purposes.* This result gives you the worst of two worlds: on one hand, the restrictions are ignored for valuation purposes; on the other hand, you now have real estate subject to development restrictions that are fully enforceable under state law. Put another way, the value is reduced but the tax is not reduced.

What all this means is that if you are going to use restrictions as part of your land and tax planning, *you should either use restrictions that meet the requirements of the tax code conservation easement rules or you shouldn't impose any restrictions.*

8. *"Leveraging Acquisition Dollars": getting more for the dollars when governments or non-profits are buying land for conservation purposes and/or when you are selling.*

Some people who work for government agencies think that the only way to control a piece of land is to buy it or to regulate it by zoning. Others have come to understand that it is possible to protect land by purchasing (or receiving by gift) a conservation easement. In fact, purchasing a conservation easement instead of purchasing the land itself is one way for governments or non-profits to "leverage" dollars that have been appropriated or raised for open space or land acquisition programs.

However, I believe there is a great deal more that government or non-profit "buyers" can do to leverage any dollars that might be available for acquisition programs. The easiest way to do this is to *make certain the seller understands all the tax planning options that are available,* or put another way, by *doing the tax planning for the seller.* If you can show the seller how to do the planning to make the purchase price go further, as the buyer you can stretch those same dollars. **Run the numbers!**

The purpose of this note in the *Appendix* is not to spend a lot of time on how to leverage acquisition dollars; the purpose of this note is to get governments and non-profit buyers to begin thinking about this interesting and important planning issue. Let me give you one example of how good tax planning *for the seller* can help close a deal.

Let's say that Farmer Brown owns a large and important tract of agricultural land in an area where agricultural land is fast becoming a dwindling resource. Let's also say the County has money to acquire high-priced agricultural land and sell or lease it back to the farming community rather than seeing it paved over and subdivided. Let's say that Farmer Brown has $1 million worth of that agricultural land he purchased many years ago, and that the County has expressed an interest in buying Farmer Brown's land but has only $500,000 available for that purpose.

Instead of selling half (or all) of his land to the County, paying a big capital gains tax on the sale, and then potentially paying estate tax on what's left of that amount when he dies, what if Farmer Brown and the County do it this way instead. What if Farmer Brown sets up a **charitable remainder trust**, deeds half of his land to the CRT, and then the CRT sells that land to the County. The CRT pays no tax, and let's say that under the terms of the CRT Farmer Brown and his wife receive a payout of 6% annually for the rest of their lives. Let's also say that Farmer Brown and his wife establish a trust to purchase some **second-to-die life insurance**. This is planning that we have already covered in *Chapter 6*.

But let's add another step. Let's also say that once the CRT has been set up and the sale to the County is complete, Farmer Brown and his wife *designate the local land trust as the charitable remainder beneficiary of the CRT.* And *then* let's say that the local land trust *acquires an option from Farmer and Mrs. Brown* to purchase the balance of the Browns' important agricultural land from their estate for its appraised estate tax value!

At some point in the future, this is what is likely to happen. Farmer Brown and Mrs. Brown die; the money in the **charitable remainder**

trust is paid to the local land trust; the local land trust buys the rest of the Browns' property from their estate. The County's purchase money has been leveraged, the agricultural land is protected, and the Brown family is happy.

This is only one example. Governments and non-profit buyers should begin to think carefully about *leveraging acquisition dollars by educating sellers about tax planning opportunities.*

9. Can a real estate developer get an income tax deduction for donating a conservation easement to protect open space in a development project?

There are three reasons why it is difficult for a real estate developer to get an income tax deduction for donating a conservation easement.

The first reason is the so-called *quid pro quo* rule. In many real estate development projects around the country, the developer will say to the planning board, or the zoning commission, or whatever the appropriate regulatory body may be, "If you let me put houses on 40% of my property, I promise that the other 60% will remain in open space." Now, there's nothing wrong with this, and it happens all the time, but *this is not a deductible charitable contribution.* This is a *quid pro quo* in a business setting: you give me this and I'll give you that.

Similarly, if a regulatory body approves a development plan, and the terms of that plan say, "You can put houses on 60% of this property, but the other 40% must remain in open space," that is a required condition of approval, and the conservation easement on that open space is not a deductible charitable contribution.

Assuming a real estate developer can get by the *quid pro quo* hurdle, another tax code rule presents a formidable obstacle. Very simply put, the tax rules say that if you are in the business of making a product and selling that product to customers, if you donate that product to charity you can take an income tax deduction but the deduction is *limited to your cost or basis of that product,* not its fair market value. In other words, say Sally's Specialties makes flouncy little pillows and sells them to customers for $39.95 each. If Sally's Specialties instead donates a dozen pillows to the local hospital, the company can take a charitable contribution deduction for *its cost* of making the pillows, not the $39.95 each it sells them for. Keep in mind that this rule doesn't mean the gift is not deductible, it only limits the *amount* of the deduction.

The same rule applies to a real estate developer who holds land and lots in inventory and sells that land to customers. If the developer donates a house lot to charity, or donates an easement on a portion of the current real estate development, the gift *may be* deductible but the deduction will be *limited to the developer's cost or basis of the lot or the easement.* (The rules for determining the basis of the easement are beyond the scope of this book.)

The third hurdle is the "conservation purposes" test imposed by the tax rules. Recall in *Chapter 4* I noted that you must protect important conservation values to meet the tax law easement requirements. In many real estate developments, the land use plan contemplates residential housing around a certain amount of "common" open space. An example would be a number of houses built around a 20-acre "park" or common area. While this might be lovely open space, and it might be a lovely amenity for the development, it isn't clear in this case that anyone other than the homeowners can enjoy the open space and it isn't clear whether any significant conservation values are being protected. Recall, too, the discussion on page 32 about why an easement on nineteen 5-acre house lots on a 100-acre piece of land probably would not meet the conservation purposes test. Certainly, there might be other similar examples in which the conservation benefits are clearer, but the point is that in many real estate developments the conservation values and benefits of a proposed conservation easement *may not be sufficient* for the easement to meet the tax rules for deductibility.

What this all means is that it is difficult at best for a real estate developer to take advantage of the tax incentives for a deductible conservation easement. Certainly, in many situations that I'm aware of, when developers have not thought about the possibility of a deductible conservation easement until *part way through a development project* it is too late: either the regulatory body has already been approached with open space as an integral part of the project (and subject to the *quid pro quo* rule), or the basis limitation rules apply, or the conservation purposes test simply isn't met.

I do believe that *in some circumstances*, with comprehensive planning, it *may be possible* for a developer to get a deduction for donating a conservation easement. Some of the important requirements are that (1) the plan to conserve must be clear from the outset; (2) the conservation purposes of the gift must be clear; (3) the open space or conservation easement cannot be a required part of the regulatory scheme; (4) the planning must be done very carefully; and (5) under the best of circumstances, the planning must begin even before the developer signs the agreement to purchase the property.

10. *What about corporate landowners? Can they donate easements? How does the charitable contribution deduction work for corporations?*

A corporation that owns land can donate an easement. All of the tax law requirements for deductibility are the same (the conservation purposes test, etc.). The biggest difference is that when a corporation makes a charitable contribution, the gift is deductible generally *up to 10% of the corporation's taxable income for the year, with a five-year carryforward of any unused amount.* Recall from *Chapter 4* that when an individual makes a contribution of an easement the gift is deductible up to 30% of that individual's income for the year, also with a five-year carryforward.

A few observations. First, if long ago Mom and Pop put the family farm into a corporation for purposes of giving shares of stock to the children (recall the warning in *Chapter 5 **never*** to do that), and the family farm runs at a modest profit if it makes a profit at all, the income tax benefits from donating a conservation easement may be very limited. In addition, the donation of a conservation easement by a family corporation with a number of shareholders (or a trust with a number of beneficiaries) can potentially raise complex legal and fiduciary responsibility questions; if you are in this situation, check with your advisors.

On the other hand, the estate tax benefits of a corporate easement in this situation may still be significant. Consider this example. Mom and Pop own all the stock of Farm Corp., and the only asset of Farm Corp. is an operating farm with real estate that has a value of $1,500,000. The stock of Farm Corp. is also worth $1,500,000, and *Mom and Pop may have an estate tax problem.* If an easement on the farm reduces the value of the real estate to $750,000, for example, the value of the stock is also reduced to $750,000. In other words, even though the income tax benefits for Mom and Pop of donating an easement may be negligible, in this case the estate tax benefits can be an important part of the planning process.

The analysis is completely different if the corporation is a large and profitable business that includes land among its many assets. In fact, I believe that many corporations should be taking a careful look at donating conservation easements on land they hold, not just for the land protection and income tax benefit opportunities but *for the potential financial benefit to the shareholders.*

Many corporations own generally undeveloped land that is somehow related to the business of the corporation. Forestland that is owned to provide a supply of forest products, including newsprint, is one good example. Many corporations own land that is not necessarily important to the current business of the corporation but that costs money to "carry on the books" each year. Many corporate landowners own land as investment, held against the distant and speculative possibility that there will be appreciation and development potential at some point in the future. With maintenance, upkeep, liability insurance, property taxes, and other carrying costs, even holding "productive" real estate can be expensive. Corporate landowners should compare the "present value" of (1) donating a deductible conservation easement on a particular tract of land and investing the income tax savings now, with (2) the *speculative* possibility of some financial gain from the sale of that land *well into the future.* In many situations, running the numbers like this can make the option of donating a conservation easement a very attractive *financial option* for a corporation. **Run the numbers!**

ABOUT THE AUTHOR

Stephen J. Small is a tax attorney at his own firm, the Law Office of Stephen J. Small, Esq., in Boston. He is the author of *The Federal Tax Law of Conservation Easements* (Land Trust Alliance, 1985) and *Preserving Family Lands* (2nd edition, Landowner Planning Center, 1992). *Preserving Family Lands* has sold more than 75,000 copies.

Before going into private practice, Mr. Small was an attorney-advisor in the Office of Chief Counsel of the Internal Revenue Service in Washington, D.C., where he wrote the federal income tax regulations on conservation easements.

Mr. Small advises landowners on federal income and estate tax planning to help preserve valued family land, including planning for the next generation of ownership. He has worked with private landowners around the country to preserve a wide range of property, from small family parcels, timberland, and dairy farms to western ranches, Atlantic coast barrier islands, farmland, and wildlife habitat.

Mr. Small has given more than one hundred fifty speeches, seminars, and workshops around the country on tax planning for landowners, succession planning for family lands, and tax incentives for land conservation. He is a member of the Massachusetts and District of Columbia Bars.

Preserving Family Lands: Book II
MORE PLANNING STRATEGIES FOR THE FUTURE

Order Form
Please cut along line at left and enclose with your check

You can order **Preserving Family Lands: Book II** as follows:

Single Copy Orders:
Preserving Family Lands: Book II @$14.95 per copy (includes postage and handling)

Bulk Orders:

30-99	@$6.00, plus shipping and handling
100 or more	@$5.00, plus shipping and handling

Shipping and Handling for bulk orders:

30-50 copies	$30.00
51-99 copies	$40.00
100-150 copies	$50.00
151-200 copies	$60.00

Please call 617-357-1644 for shipping charges for quantities over 200.

☐ I would like to order _____ copies of **Preserving Family Lands: Book II**
at $ _____ per copy.
Total dollar amount for copies ordered   _____
Shipping and handling charges (bulk orders only)   _____
5% MA Sales Tax (for orders shipped to Massachusetts addresses)   _____
                         TOTAL: _____

Please send to the following address:

Name: _____

Affiliation or Business (if applicable): _____

Street: _____

City, State, Zip Code: _____

Please Note: We ship by UPS. If you are ordering more than ten (10) copies, please use a street address since UPS will NOT deliver to a Post Office Box.

A CHECK FOR THE FULL AMOUNT MUST ACCOMPANY YOUR ORDER.
Please make check out to "Preserving Family Lands" and mail to:

> Preserving Family Lands
> PO Box 2242
> Boston, MA 02107

☐ Please send me an order form for *Preserving Family Lands* (Book I)

Prices may be subject to change